Anger
at Work

Also by Hendrie Weisinger, Ph.D.

Nobody's Perfect

Dr. Weisinger's Anger Work-out Book

*The Critical Edge: How to Criticize Up and Down Your
Organization and Make It Pay Off*

Anger
at Work

Hendrie Weisinger, Ph.D.

WILLIAM MORROW AND COMPANY, INC.
New York

It is the policy of William Morrow and Company, Inc., and its imprints and affiliates, recognizing the importance of preserving what has been written, to print the books we publish on acid-free paper, and we exert our best efforts to that end.

Library of Congress Cataloging-in-Publication Data

Weisinger, Hendrie.
    Anger at work / Hendrie Weisinger. — 1st ed.
      p.   cm.
    Includes bibliographical references and index.
    ISBN 0-688-12018-0
    1. Conflict management. 2. Anger. 3. Interpersonal conflict.
4. Self-perception. I. Title.
HD42.W437   1995
650.1'3—dc20
                                    94-42143
                                      CIP

Printed in the United States of America

First Edition

1 2 3 4 5 6 7 8 9 10

BOOK DESIGN BY PATRICE SHERIDAN

Acknowledgments

There are many people to acknowledge, all of whom were supportive and encouraging, and many of whom contributed their valuable insights and expertise to the writing of this book. Because there are so many, I will keep my thanks short.

It is appropriate to start with Ron Podell for suggesting and encouraging me to write *Anger at Work* and for throwing in the title, too. I would like to acknowledge Kenny Cinnamon for his tremendously creative and original thoughts and his desire to see me succeed; Consigliere Lenny Levine, who gives my family protection on the Coast, teaches Dantino the casino business, and takes care of his older brother; and The Fabulous One, Alan Driefuss, for always making those long drives and reminding me to slow down: Your friendship is greater than number NY 7. Wess Roberts helped me sort through loads of data at warp speed to generate the most anger-provoking situations. Believe me, only a great friend would do that.

Thanks go to Robert Braun for providing a home away from home, and to Mel Kinder, who, despite wanting his own family,

proved to be a loyal button man by offering help with the flap—
Cinnamon greatly improved it.

My friend Howard Norman provides me with opportunities
whenever he can and, I am proud to say, has taken a true interest
in my career. Robert Barron, friend, colleague, and partner: You
are the true expert on positive affect, and your social psychology
book served as a primary source. You always breathe "fresh air"
into work and know the sweet smell of success. You gave me the
aggression paper just in time. Terry Schmidt always sends me the
books I miss and is always trying to give me unlimited power.
Kenny Shapiro, an old buddy, has always taken the time from his
busy days to run to the post office to send me things I should
know about. He knows the Point. Kelsey Tyson, whom I have
missed, is back in the picture, and already makes me feel more
confident.

My friends at UCLA Executive Education and Engineering
Management have been a tremendous source of support and encouragement over the years. Darwin Eads, an old friend and colleague and an expert in the art of incompletes, is always good for
advice and support. Elaine Hadfield, the acknowledged expert on
emotional contagion, provided me with the material I needed
and deserves great recognition for her groundbreaking work. Jess
Bedolla is a great encourager who knows how important criticism
and anger are—especially if you are a Dodger fan. Thanks go to
Tom Evonick for knowing how to use the mail to say hi and for
knowing Connecticut was the right move.

Lee Sachs, who knows quality and value, is a most valued
friend. His advice on all phases of life has added wise perspective
to my life. Viva La Villa!

Thanks are due to Albert Roberts, a new friend and colleague,
who has already trusted me with his class, and to my sister Joyce
for being the pathfinder. Gordon Peters and my IMS friends have
continued to believe in my work and have provided numerous
opportunities for me to get it to corporate America. I look forward
to coming to Reno. I thank Dick Zief for his interest and enthu-

siasm for my work and for turning me on to some good Chinese restaurants.

To my nephews, Derek and Randy, for learning how to manage their anger when the Wolverines frequently lose the big ones, when the Yankees win, and when I defeat them in all types of encounters—I'm very proud of you. Randy, do your job! Thanks to Don and Ronnie for their continual support, to Steve Gold for knowing that no drive is too far when there is a good purpose, and to Ray Burrasca for beginning the Westport regime and for being a valuable member of the Family.

Thanks to the folks at William Morrow for doing it again: to Andy Dutter for getting it started and to Toni Sciarra for shepherding it through. Also, I thank Tory Klose for editing wisely.

My mother, Thelma, has given unselfishly of herself and has always been able to help me manage my anger. She's still mommy to me.

My wife, Lorie, has proved to be an unlimited reservoir of enthusiasm, energy, and love.

There are many others, but I will send them copies of this book instead of taking up more space. They understand and all know how much I appreciate their support and efforts on my behalf. Thank you all. Manage your anger.

Contents

Anger
at Work

Introduction

Anger. It's in the world. Always has been. Always will be. It's a universal experience that transcends time, cultures, and species. Dogs get angry. So do bees. And so does anybody who works.

This book is about the experience of anger in the context of work and how that experience affects your thoughts, your feelings, the way you act. It is also a book about what you can do to influence your anger episodes and how you can use them to enhance more than your job results—your work experience—in multiple and diverse ways.

You don't have to be a psychologist to know that managing anger productively is something few individuals, organizations, and societies do well. Your own observations and knowledge will prove this to be true, especially in your work environment.

Yet there is a plethora of empirical research indicating that individuals who do manage their anger at work are much more successful than those who don't. The sales rep, for example, who uses the anger provoked by a last-minute canceled order as a source of energy to call other customers is sure to outperform his counterpart who lets his anger ruin his day. The manager who is able to control her emotions when riled by an abrasive executive puts herself in a better light than her colleague who in the same situation sheds tears or explodes.

The co-worker who can productively confront his teammate about his substandard performance and negative attitude increases his group's chances for success as well as minimizes the destructive conflicts that arise when such confrontations are mishandled. The customer service agent who can defuse the angry customer not only keeps her customers loyal, but also makes her own day a lot less troublesome. The executive who knows how to help her managers use anger to transform an "angry" organization into an enthusiastic one will see profits.

All of these people go home a lot healthier.

People who manage their anger at work do have an edge, a very crucial one. Giving you this edge is the first objective of *Anger at Work.*

The second objective is to expand your awareness of the role emotions, feelings, and moods play in the business environment. Again, there is an abundance of recent research that shows these factors—typically thought to be of little significance—can greatly affect the course of the business day for better or worse.

Obviously, those skilled in using these life components advantageously will increase their edge in many ways. They will be able, for instance, to relate to others more effectively, thus restoring some of the interpersonal connectedness that seems to be lacking for too many these days, something that contributes to burnout. They will know how to stop the spread of negative emotions that permeate a lot of organizations. And they will be able to infect themselves and their fellow workers with positive emotions—antidotes to low morale, feelings of being overwhelmed, and obstacles to success that seem to crop up every other day. These skills increase in value and pay strong dividends too.

ANGER AND WORK: WHY THEY
GO TOGETHER

Much can be said about the psychology of work, but for our purposes we need only to state:

1. Work is a primary way for expressing yourself—your interests, your skills, your thoughts, and your creativity.
2. Work is a principal means of validating your self-esteem. Success at work usually translates into feeling good about yourself, while failure has the reverse effect.
3. Work is a principal means of helping you meet many of your psychological and biological needs, including the need to be recognized, the need to be competent, the need to belong, and economic needs.
4. Working in meaningful activities is a well-validated trait of the healthy individual, and work lacking in purpose creates feelings of anger, depression, and despair.

Taken together, these four working propositions make it easy to see why anger and work go together.

During the natural run of a workday, events occur that take us off course from integrating the psychological currents of work with our job activities; for example, a performance appraisal perceived to be below standard prevents you from having your self-esteem need met as well as threatens your (economic) security needs.

Many times, these workday events are out of our control—a layoff, a favorite boss gets fired, the company moves its plant. Other times, these incidents prevent us from experiencing the psychological payoffs of work. When this happens—when our needs are endangered, when we perceive we are victims of a situation that is beyond control—we become angry, as one of anger's many functions is to help us get our needs met and potentiate feelings of control.

Simply stated, the nature of work naturally provokes anger. And believe me, it doesn't matter whether your job is being the president of the United States, an NFL quarterback, a teacher, an FBI agent, a director or actor, doctor or nurse, real estate agent, stockbroker, or truck driver. No matter what type of work you do, there will be events that provoke your anger because they threaten your needs and/or are beyond your area of control. Comes with the job. Any job. Couple this with the fact that most people manage anger ineffectively, and it's easy to understand why so many people report so many episodes of anger on the job.

WHAT IS ANGER?: A DIMENSIONAL VIEW

There is a tremendous amount of literature in the area of anger. Psychology alone has at least a dozen major avenues of thought and research on the subject. Sociologists, anthropologists, cardiologists, physiologists, biologists, and chemists represent only a fraction of the different bodies of knowledge that have delved into the study of anger, each with its own definition.

It is only after continually studying this information, and only after having fifteen years of experience in applied anger management in settings that include *Fortune* 500 companies; government agencies; school systems; mental health agencies; hospitals; marriage, family, and individual therapy; and my own experiences that I am able to comfortably proclaim myself an angerologist with expertise in anger management. So being, I have found that the best way to define anger is phenomenologically—do it for yourself. You've seen it, and felt it, and spoken it. And I know you have acted on it. Rather than try to give you a definition, I will simply assume that when we speak of anger, you can relate to the experience.

My interest and goal is to help you understand and develop the skills of anger management. To achieve this end, I have found it most useful to conceptualize anger as consisting of five inter-related dimensions all operating simultaneously in any anger experience. These dimensions are:

1. Cognition: our current thoughts
2. Emotion: the physiological arousal that anger generates
3. Communication: how we let others know we are angry
4. Affect: how we experience the world when we are angry
5. Behavior: how we act when we are angry

While each dimension is a crucial determinant in how anger of the moment is managed, and while there will be times when one dimension takes precedence over the others, remember that any one dimension is always influencing the others and vice versa. For example, what you think while you are angry influences how you feel; how you feel when you are angry influences how you communicate; how you communicate affects how you think; how you think affects how you behave.

The art of anger management—being able to transform anger from a negative experience into a positive one—is developed by knowing how to use each dimension of anger and how to blend them together so that they work for you. It is my goal to help you learn this.

STRESS AND ANGER: WHAT'S THE RELATIONSHIP?

Like anger, stress is a subject that has been dealt with widely. No doubt you are familiar with the term *stress management*. While there are similarities, stress and anger are not the same, and anger management should not be confused with the concept of stress management.

Stress is best thought of as a condition in which there is an imbalance between situational demands and resources to respond. Getting three letters out, attending two meetings, returning a bunch of phone calls, signing off on a budget, and having to do it all in an afternoon can be a stressful situation if you perceive you do not have the means to react to all. Certainly, you have options. You can prioritize, delegate, laugh about it, blow some of it off, get anxious, become depressed, or become angry. In this context, stress management refers to how you handle the demands made upon you by, for example, using time management skills.

Anger can be a reaction to stress. Screaming at your kids when they ask you to play with them while you are trying to get some last-minute work done is a familiar example of how we respond to stressful situations with anger. But anger can also be generated in situations that do not tax your resources. Harassment and violation of trust provoke anger, but the anger is not a reaction to stress per se. As such, anger must be considered more specific and broader than the concept of stress. More specific in that it has unique physiological, cognitive, and behavioral correlates; broader in that it is an emotion and a feeling. Anger management refers to how you control the experience of anger so that it works for you. Time management, for example, is not an anger management skill.

Stress can evoke anger, but to be under stress is not to be angry—you could be depressed—and to be angry certainly does not mean you are stressed out.

WHAT TO EXPECT

Anger at Work is organized into eight chapters. The first focuses on the concept of self-awareness, a factor crucial in determining how well you can manage anger. The next five chapters detail each dimension of anger. Many specifics and a summary of each chapter will highlight key concepts. The seventh chapter, "Anger in Motion," is a case study that will allow you to assess your anger management knowledge. The eighth chapter, "The Art of Anger Management," illustrates the creative and effective application of anger management concepts and skills to the most anger-provoking occurrences on the job, situations and issues I have identified over fifteen years by listening to thousands of working people in diverse work settings. Managing angry people, coping with the harassing boss or unfair performance appraisals, and lack of teamwork are only a few of the anger provokers that appear to be timeless and ones that inevitably we all encounter.

Key points drawn from these situations will provide you with a generic model for practicing the art of anger management. Profits, both professional and personal, will result.

Anger and
Self-awareness

I will always remember the TV producer who told me about presenting a script for a new series to a vice president of a Big Three network. With his writing staff, the producer waited expectantly, hoping for praise and encouragement, as the script was the result of months of work. But the reaction from the vice president was anger. "This script is *ridiculous*," he yelled with a red face. "Nothing fresh. Same old stuff. Now I am very disappointed. I had the network psyched up and you gave me something that is so bad it will probably not even be able to be shredded." Then with thick sarcasm, he added, "How long have you been in the business?"

A few days later, still feeling bitter, the producer bumped into the executive on the studio lot and asked what he had hoped to accomplish with such destructive, angry remarks. The vice president was astonished. He simply hadn't realized how he was coming off. In fact, he adamantly denied he had been harsh. And he wasn't just being defensive: He actually believed he wasn't angry.

The vice president's reaction should not come as a surprise; it doesn't to me. I have heard thousands of similar stories with the proverbial tag line "Oh really? Gee, I guess I wasn't aware I was acting like that."

Contrary to the perceptions most people hold of themselves, it is the rare individual who possesses high self-awareness—having an accurate understanding of how he behaves or of how other people know him; recognizing how he responds to others; and being sensitive to his attitudes, feelings, emotions, and general communication style.

Self-awareness is crucial to effective functioning because it brings into clarity how you operate, thereby giving you valuable data that can help you be more effective.

Your self is the center of your universe. The subjective knowledge you have about the nature of your personality not only guides your behavior from situation to situation, but also provides you with the larger framework for making sense out of your life. It is through your own perceptions that you determine and explain your life results, whether you make yourself a hero, villain, or victim. Those with high self-awareness are able to make exact interpretations of their life events and use them to further their pursuits, whether it's a job promotion or a more meaningful relationship.

With low self-awareness, your actions are handicapped by incomplete and inaccurate information, factors that guarantee failure. Specifically, low self-awareness blinds you to how other people see you, distorts your self-perceptions, causes you to act maladaptively, and prevents you from learning about yourself. In a business context, low self-awareness is an impetus for poor decision making, ineffective communication, and lack of sensitivity to fellow workers, and it stagnates your professional growth. Indeed, it has been my observation that individuals who possess low self-awareness are not successful.

High self-awareness is the focal point for managing anger because the use of anger management skills presupposes that you know when you are angry and, more important, recognize when you are becoming angry, thus allowing you to quickly use anger's primary function—as a cue that something is wrong. The sales rep who feels his anger fever up in response to a difficult client gives himself the chance to control that anger and generate a productive response instead. Those who are oblivious to what anger's initial stages feel like are more apt to explode, later reporting that "it just happened," as if they were struck by lightning out of the blue. The sales rep who fails to recognize his client's anger pertaining to a canceled appointment not only misses the opportunity to amend the situation quickly, but increases the likelihood of repeating the act and, eventually, losing the client.

The first action, then, that I recommend is to begin the process of increasing your self-awareness by developing what I call "positive self-consciousness."

In contrast to being self-conscious, a term traditionally used to describe those who are ill at ease and usually ineffective, positive self-consciousness refers to the ability to continually monitor how you act, feel, and think and to be able to use this information to become more effective in responding to the situations at hand. Successful people, whether at work or at home, are typically skilled in positive self-consciousness.

Acquiring positive self-consciousness does not require hundreds of hours of psychotherapy. What it does require, however, is some thoughtfulness and some time, and inevitably the courage to deal with how you actually react to the events and people in your life.

Begin simply. Pay attention to the basics—how you think, how you feel, and how you respond. For example, focus on your thoughts when in different situations. The next time you are stuck in traffic, getting ready for your weekend golf game, or find yourself losing your cool with a subordinate, listen to the thoughts that fill your mind. Are they helpful or making matters worse?

Instead of telling yourself that your boss's appraisal is unfair, provoking you to respond with anger, ask yourself to find out the rationale for his statements and respond by listening, an important anger communication skill.

By monitoring these basics in different situations, you will gradually achieve positive self-consciousness and be able to effectively and intentionally use your thoughts to manage anger-provoking events. The same will be true for your feelings, emotions, behavior, and how you communicate at any particular time, especially when you are angry. When you're being chewed out by a client, your heartbeat speeds up. Missing that cue permits your emotions to boil, but sensing it reminds you to manage your anger by breathing slower and to use your thoughts productively. You will probably find it helpful to put some visual cues (e.g., a three- by five-inch index card on your desk that says THOUGHTS, FEELINGS, BEHAVIOR) in your surroundings to remind you to monitor yourself.

I also want you to increase your self-awareness because a significant amount of recent empirical research (to be discussed later) indicates that your moods and feelings and those of others have a great effect on how you perform at work.

As you become more aware of your immediate feelings and moods and of those of the people you work with, you will be able to apply some of the current psychological technologies that focus on improving performance by influencing moods and feelings. For now, gather "mood information" by examining your sensitivity to moods and feelings. Do you know, for instance, when your subordinates are anxious? Do you know when your boss is depressed? How do you tell if your co-worker is angry or sad?

What about you? Are you aware of how you act when you feel anxious? What differences do you note about yourself when you are enthused or bored? When was the last time you noticed a subordinate was upset—and what did you do?

The importance of increasing your self-awareness and achieving positive self-consciousness cannot be overstated. It is the prerequisite to managing anger as well as to improving your overall functioning. Therefore, I would strongly recommend that you begin the process immediately.

Key Concepts: Implicit in managing anger is being aware of when you are angry and how you respond. Positive self-consciousness gives you the information necessary to decide the best way of responding to maximize your results. You can attain positive self-consciousness by focusing on how you feel, act, and think in various circumstances, especially ones in which you are angry. As you gain a greater awareness of yourself, you will be able to conduct yourself more productively.

Anger and Cognition

This chapter focuses on the relationship between anger and cognition with the intention of showing you how to utilize specific cognitive processes to manage your anger experiences.

COGNITIVE PROCESSES

Imagine the following situation: You are sitting in your office checking your expense account and your thoughts turn to an experience you had the day before. You were in a meeting with a group of ten people, and your boss entered the room. Without any salutations, he looked at you sternly and said harshly, "John, that report was terrible. Come into my office as soon as you are finished." As he left the room, your face was flushed with anger.

You quickly scanned your co-workers and noted that each one was avoiding your look. Even though you knew you were about to face your boss's wrath, you were relieved when the meeting was adjourned. You were the first one out of the room, but over-heard a few of your colleagues' sympathies.

Now, as you think back over your boss's surly behavior, you feel your pulse quicken. Soon, you are experiencing intense anger all over again.

Situations like this suggest that cognitive processes—our cur-rent thoughts—frequently exert strong effects on our emotional states. Indeed, as this example illustrates, your thoughts are ca-pable of generating emotional reactions that are fully as intense as those produced by external causes (e.g., events we experience, the words or deeds of others). To extrapolate, what you think and how you think influence your experience of anger.

It is also true that anger affects your thinking. Memory, crea-tivity, and concentration weaken. Your thoughts become accu-satory, exaggerated, rigid. You treat your assumptions as facts; you often become irrational.

Cognitive Appraisal: Evaluating Your Thoughts

Cognitive appraisal is the mental process that helps you define and interpret what is happening to or around you. Its roots lie in special qualities and circumstances—family background, natural talents, physical appearance, systems of belief—that help shape your personality. These combine to form the basis for the unique way you appraise the situations you encounter in daily life. Through cognitive appraisal, you generate the self-statements and expectations that help guide your behavior.

Anger and cognitive appraisal are related in two key ways: The first, and more general way, is based on the premise that the way you appraise your environment at any given moment is crucial in determining how you respond. The second is underlined by the fact that there are broad styles of thinking that actually create anger. Furthermore, the experience of anger prompts these thinking styles to be used. By sharpening your cognitive appraisals, you can make the first point work for you and rid yourself of the anger associated with the second.

A Cognitive Perspective

If you appraise your boss's negative reaction to a project as a reflection of his jealousy or insecurity, you are apt to respond with anger. A very different response would result if you interpreted his remarks as being based on valid research that could enhance your report.

While this point is hardly original (Epictetus said two thousand years ago, "Men are not troubled by things themselves, but by their thoughts about them"), today psychologists agree that it is the meaning we assign to events that gives them the power to affect us for good or ill.

Many times we find ourselves repetitively responding to the same event or person with anger. The event may be a flat tire or a foul-up with a photocopying machine. The person may be your abrasive boss or a co-worker who sloughs off. Because you always respond with anger in these instances, it seems natural to think that the event itself makes you angry. Indeed, I have found that when individuals state that someone or something "made" them angry, it is not a conscious attempt to avoid responsibility but an accurate reflection of their own experience. In their minds, they are victims forced into destructive outbursts.

Alas, the culprit is *not* the event; it is the interpretation of the event. The best the incident can do is to trigger your anger, not make you angry. In other words, when you say that something makes you angry, you are acknowledging that anger is your habitual response to the event; you are not able or do not know how to respond to the situation or person differently. These instances—the ones you habitually answer with anger—are called provocations; they provoke your anger response.

The importance of this cognitive perspective of anger is that it empowers you by putting you in control. Anger becomes your choice rather than some automatic response you are powerless to inhibit ("I couldn't control myself") or something thrust upon you ("It just happened").

Accordingly, cognitive appraisal is the process that allows you to evaluate provocations more accurately, to look at them from other perspectives, to realize your options. With these thoughts, you can then decide whether an anger response is the best reaction to the situation or if—and what is usually the case—you have to choose another response that will enable you to deal more effectively with the provoking situation.

THE ANGER RESPONSE—WHEN TO CHOOSE IT

There are many times when anger is beneficial. In the context of coping with loss, for example, anger protects the individual from experiencing a harsher reality—and gradually diminishes as the individual is able to confront the situation. But we aim to explore when to *choose* anger as an effective response for productive gains. I can offer you a few guidelines I have found to be useful in appraising when anger is apt to be an effective response.

Anger is an effective response when it helps you change a situation that is unjust. Whether the provocation is unjust is open to debate, so you will find it useful to always have a frame of reference to help you decide this. I instruct people to quickly ask themselves—or others when possible—in any anger-provoking circumstance, "Would others think this is unjust?" If you reflect on this question and your answer is yes, you are likely to feel more comfortable with your anger knowing that you're not alone in your thinking. Discrimination, harassment, and invalid performance ratings are only a few of the provocations that, according

to thousands of people in the working world, are unjust and wor-
thy of an anger response. In these cases, anger helps because it
can supply you with the emotional energy to cope with and pursue
the provocation until resolution.

Anger is also a helpful response when you have been intentionally hurt by others. Did the person do this on purpose or was
it an accident or company procedure? Being maligned by a co-
worker's rumor, being verbally abused by boss or client, or being
lied to are all intentional acts that call for an anger response.
Your anger response will potentiate a feeling of control that will
not only serve the function of instigating you to confront the
provoking individual, but also help you feel more comfortable
(more in control) during a confrontation. It's been my observation that for most individuals, whether they are in the executive
ranks or in the blue-collar trenches, acts of confrontation and
criticism are extremely anxiety arousing. The usual response
tends to be one of avoidance, which merely perpetuates the situation, thereby causing an increase in anger levels.

These are the only two specific circumstances when an anger
response seems to be beneficial. This is not to say that it is im-
proper to get angry in other instances—anger is a feeling and an
emotion and it is part of the human existence, thus making it
your inherent right to experience it.

But this does not mean that responding with anger is always
your best choice. A time-wasting meeting, a failing fax machine,
and a missed phone call are frequently anger-provoking events.
Nevertheless, in these cases, your anger response is likely to make
the situation worse by clouding your judgment in determining
your best line of action. For sure, a strategically posed question
that stimulates thought and puts an end to a time-wasting meeting is a more effective response than an outburst of "This is a
waste of time" or sitting to a slow boil.

To assess the effectiveness of anger in these and all other circumstances, I suggest asking yourself the following question
whenever you experience anger (your answer will help you deter-

mine if anger is your best choice of response): "Is my anger helping me or hurting me?"

When the answer is "helping," it's a cue that you're on the
right track to making anger work for you. You're probably using
your anger to resolve a conflict; you're using your anger adaptively. When the answer is "hurting," it's a message that your
anger is needless; it is making the situation worse. In these instances, it's time to respond differently.

Key Concepts: Events have no emotional meaning per se: It is
your interpretation of these events, how you appraise them, that
creates the anger response. With this frame of mind, anger becomes a choice, and to use anger productively you must be able
to judge if it is the best response to a provoking event. One time
that it is never your best choice is when your anger is the result
of a distorted thinking style.

Distorted Thinking Styles

The second way anger and cognitive appraisal are related centers
on the concept of distorted thinking styles—habitual ways of
thinking that cause a misperception. Like sunglasses, they color
your perceptions of the world (some of the world might be red
but not all of it). These misperceptions are typically loaded
with specific self-statements that are anger-provoking in nature
and that, consequently, can create anger. Because these self-
statements are based on distorted perceptions of reality, the anger
is always needless and never useful. If you continually use the
same distorted thinking styles, you will develop the habit of using
the same self-statements.

Often, cognitive distortions characterize an individual's general thinking style. For these people, we could accurately predict
that they are frequently angry and their job performance is impeded.

It is also important to note that the experience of anger in itself often prompts a distorted thinking style. When you are angry, for example, your thinking becomes rigid, thus causing you to think of a situation in a particular way that blots out all other options and explanations, which could help you deal with the provocation more effectively. As you become angrier and more emotional, your thinking becomes much more rigid. This rigid thinking increases the likelihood that your perceptions of reality begin to distort the situation. These distorted thoughts then become part of your momentary thinking and go on to intensify the anger experience, prompting more distorted perceptions to occur. The anger that was initially appropriate to the event has become inappropriate and needless because it is making the situation worse.

To illustrate, suppose you receive notice that a project has been canceled after you had been promised the green light. Based on that promise, you had already made commitments to others. To top it off, you find out that your boss knew the project was dead several weeks before he told you. Most people would have little trouble acknowledging they would become angry in such a situation. But unless that anger is managed, your thinking is apt to become distorted. Looking to explain the situation, you start to believe that your boss delayed telling you because the real intent was to make you look bad. Now you are really boiling. Next, you tell yourself that your job is in jeopardy; the best you can expect is a poor performance evaluation. As these beliefs are integrated into your thinking, your anger is apt to intensify, causing you to become hostile to those around you, especially your boss. Over time, your concentration weakens and your performance actually becomes worse. You become even angrier.

In reality, your boss's delay in notifying you was due to his last-minute efforts to rescue your project. True, he could have told you that the project was in jeopardy, but his intent was far from making you look bad. As for your job's being in danger, your boss actually believes you are a stellar performer and you are on course for an excellent performance report; that is, until your anger made the situation worse.

This is a cognitive danger of anger. Once you become angry, you can become even angrier because of the emergence of a distorted thinking style.

There are four distorted thinking styles that instigate a great amount of counterproductive anger: magnifying, destructive labeling, imperative thinking, and mind reading. My estimation is that anger thinking styles account for approximately 90 percent of the times you experience anger. Such a cognitive force deserves a little more attention.

MAGNIFYING

Magnifying is a thinking style that turns the consequences of a negative event into a catastrophe. If you usually get angry when you are two minutes late for a meeting or miss a particular phone call, you are a magnifier.

Magnifying often occurs when you are already slightly irritated and distorts your thoughts by making everything seem worse than it really is. You are actually making a mountain out of a molehill. Being a minute or two late for a meeting may be embarrassing, but it is hardly realistic to tell yourself you are going to be fired or not get the sale because of a few minutes of tardiness. Once in a blue moon, maybe, but not usually.

These exaggerated and catastrophic thoughts will intensify, as well as lengthen the duration of, your emotional reaction, way out of proportion. Before you know it, your anger is full blown—and to what purpose?

DESTRUCTIVE LABELING

Destructive labeling is an extreme form of overgeneralization. When you use destructive labeling, you broaden one or two qualities into a negative global judgment (for example, calling your boss a jerk or a client a pain in the butt).

Someone might indeed have violated your trust, and you are absolutely justified in resenting what that person did. But by making the other person totally negative, you become inappropriately indignant and morally superior. They are wrong, you are right, when, in fact, you are both right and wrong. Destructive labeling creates and perpetuates anger because it forces you to focus on only the negative characteristics you find irritating in another person. Continually thinking about these characteristics stirs up your anger, making it more and more intense until it serves only counterproductive purposes.

Sometimes people intentionally use destructive labeling to protect their own self-esteem. If we feel threatened, rejected, or disagreed with, we may engage in destructive labeling to disqualify the opponent—not a good move.

IMPERATIVE THINKING

Plato wrote in *The Republic* more than two thousand years ago that people get angry when they perceive others did not do what they ought to have done. He called this the "ought motive" for getting angry. I refer to it as imperative thinking—having a list of inflexible rules about how you and others should act. When you find other peoples' actions are not to your liking, you tell yourself they "shouldn't" do that or they "should have" done something they failed to do—"You should have called me back right away if you weren't interested" is a common example I hear from anger management seminar participants. So is "I should have been given that assignment."

Imperative thinking creates anger because it implies that we are entitled to get what we want in a specific situation or that people should be the way we want them to be. Consequently, when our imperatives are violated, we think that an injustice has taken place.

Violating our own self-requirements—"I should have done a better job"—also creates anger because we perceive the violation as failure. In reality, the violation usually reflects the fact that we did not meet our unrealistically high expectations, a trait of the chronically angry person.

MIND READING

When you presume that your project has been canceled because your boss wanted to make you look bad, you are guilty of mind reading—attributing to people motives that explain their actions to your satisfaction. Rarely do you bother to check out your presumptions, acting instead as if they were ultimately true. It is the presumption of another's deliberate malevolent intent that fuels anger and the desire for revenge. These presumptions tend to become self-fulfilling prophecies because if people do act in ways that are inconsistent with our negative presumptions, we fail to recognize it and reward them. An example of mind reading would be, "If my co-worker respected me, he would have asked for my opinion. Since he doesn't, I will ignore his input too."

Key Concepts: Perhaps you can now begin to see one of the reasons why self-awareness is so important. The more aware you are of how you think, the easier it will become to identify whether or not you are using a distorted thinking style.

When a distorted thinking style is absent, you are most likely using your anger adaptively; that is, it is helping you deal with a provocation. When a distorted thinking style is present, however, it's a cue that your anger is needless—you need less of it because it is making the situation worse. It is, therefore, important that you know how to home in on your anger distortions—the specific self-statements that create and perpetuate anger. These self-statements can then serve as a cue that you may be using a distorted thinking style and can prompt you to check out whether your anger is the response of choice.

Once you know how you think, you will be in a good position to learn how to sharpen your cognitive appraisals and combat your distorted thinking, essentials for managing anger productively.

Self-statements

Self-statements, thought talk, and *inner dialogue* are all terms that refer to what you say to yourself. They reflect your cognitive appraisals. Because these thoughts come so quickly, and because they seem to occur without any prior reasoning or reflection, they are called automatic thoughts.

Automatic thoughts have the following characteristics:

- They are private. Most people talk to themselves differently from the way they talk to others. When we talk to others, we tend to describe our life events in a rational manner. But when we talk to ourselves, we are frequently irrational and use horrifying overgeneralizations, such as "I'm going to get fired. My career is over!"
- They are almost always believed by us. Despite their irrationality, automatic thoughts are unquestioningly accepted. They seem plausible because they are hardly noticed. We don't question them or challenge them, nor are their implications logically analyzed.
- They are discrete and specific messages. They give us a direct and distinct message about some event, such as "She thinks I'm incompetent."
- They usually appear in brief form. Automatic thoughts are frequently abbreviated to one word, or a transient visual image. For example, a rising executive may say, "Zip," to tell himself that he will be left with no job after a company merger. An employee envisioning her co-worker talking to their boss may use that image to tell herself that her co-worker is getting the one promotion available.

- They are learned. Since we were born, people have been telling us what to think. Our family, friends, teachers, those we work with, and even the media condition us to appraise events in specific ways.
- They tend to be catastrophic. Automatic thoughts tend to act as cues for other thoughts. One angry thought may trigger a whole chain of angry thoughts.
- They are hard to turn off. Because automatic thoughts go undernoticed, they seem to come and go as they wish.

Here is an example of an automatic thought that typically happens when your boss expresses anger at you.

Automatic thought: "He is really upset with me."
Really means: "I am in big trouble. I am going to get fired. I won't get any references and won't be able to get another job. I will have no money to pay my bills. I will lose everything. My family will leave me. My life's a mess."

If you think that's an exaggeration, think again. I've seen this thinking pattern hundreds of times and now believe it is a frequent "thinking response" to a boss's angry expression of disappointment in an employee's work. Naturally, such self-statements make the situation worse.

MANAGING ANGER COGNITIVELY

Now is a good time to look at how you can begin to manage your cognitive processes for better anger management. Through the years of being an angerologist I have found that there is a collection of cognitive strategies and interventions that are easy to learn, can be applied quickly, and are effective in their job. I find them to be best presented in the following order:

Identifying Provocations
Alternative Explanations
Combating Anger Distortions
Anger Management Instructions
Clarifying Expectations
Mental Rehearsal

All of the interventions are based on research findings that indicate a change in your thinking changes your behavior, emotions, feelings, and moods. Because of this common denominator, they are deemed "cognitive interventions."

Before proceeding, it is a good time to remind you that all of the interventions presented throughout the book require that you turn the recommendations into actions. Remember, you don't lose weight by reading a diet book.

Identifying Provocations

Identifying your provocations helps you cognitively manage your anger because it gives you the data you need to evaluate the best way to confront or, in some cases, to avoid a provocation. Identifying a provocation is the prelude to many other anger management interventions, not just the cognitive ones. The intervention is recommended by two points.

First, the better you prepare for a situation, the more likely you will be able to generate the most effective response. Just as the star athlete readies herself by studying every move of her opponent, so identifying your provocations helps ready you by allowing you to study their nature.

Second, you have a greater chance of generating an effective response to a provocation when you are experiencing a low degree of anger arousal. With high degrees of anger arousal, you lose the ability to analyze your options. So instead of responding in a novel way that may be productive, you are apt to respond in your typical manner—with an anger response that makes the situation worse. By identifying the provocations, you can study them in the absence of anger arousal and therefore think of your best options if provoked again.

As you identify your provocations, you will note that they come in different shapes and forms. Some are "mental," manifested in the self-statements or inner dialogues you have with yourself. Others, like layoffs and strikes, are external events, while still others shape up as interpersonal, like a bad relationship with a co-worker. Knowing what shape the provocations take is important because different types of aggravations call for different anger management interventions. Managing mental provocations, for example, requires different skills from managing interpersonal ones.

Begin to identify the provocations with the simple exercise of completing the sentence "I get angry when _____." Try to get at least seven provoking events. Next to each one, write the who, what, and when of the incident and any other thoughts that help you evaluate the full nature of the provocation.

Alternative Explanations

By now you must know that the angrier you become, the more your thinking becomes mentally rigid. You often end up with "hardening of the corollaries." In this condition, you become locked into your position. It is hard to listen to others, let alone see any other option except your own. Soon you are acting counterproductively. In order to prevent such a state of mind, I recommend generating alternative explanations.

The use of alternative explanations is based on the premise that any situation (provocation) can be interpreted in multiple ways. By taking into account alternative explanations of a provoking event, you are more likely to put it in proper perspective and thereby respond much more appropriately.

An underlying feature of this intervention is that the mere generating of alternative explanations serves the function of interrupting your angry thinking, even if it is only for a second or two. This slight interruption many times will be enough to change your outlook and prevent the emergence of cognitive distortions and mental rigidity. This technique also reflects a general directive of all the cognitive interventions: Slow down your thinking when you are angry.

The subject of alternative explanations is a new one but it has already been proven to be an effective anger management intervention in at least three different types of situations: 1) When you are angry and on your own; 2) When you are involved in interpersonal conflicts; and 3) When you are around angry people and it is beneficial to change their angry moods.

You're alone on a business trip as the sole representative of your company. You're ready to make an important presentation that the client's CEO promised to attend. It is now kickoff time and she has not shown up. Your first cognitive appraisal is that the CEO never really intended to come, that you are a low priority item to her, and that you certainly cannot trust her. This explanation of her failure to attend makes you boil, and even the most competent would find it hard to give his best presentation with these thoughts as a backdrop.

You could use an alternative explanation to help yourself manage the situation. After your first anger-provoking appraisal, immediately explain the situation differently. "She must have gotten tied up in her own meeting" or "Something unexpected must have come up." Even if these are only momentary thoughts, they often do their job just by changing your perspective so you can calm down long enough to regain your composure and consider other options. This is analogous to being angry at a friend for being late until you begin to wonder if something is wrong. Your anger quickly dissipates.

Here's another example. Instead of explaining your customer's delay in giving you an order as a lack of confidence in your product or ability to deliver goods, explain the same situation from his point of view—that he needs more time to study the data or that he needs help in explaining your proposal to his superiors. While your first explanation would certainly lead to frustration and anger, the second is apt to help you explore his possible resistance and offer the help he may need to convince his boss that your proposal is the best one.

You can also use the concept of alternative explanations when you are involved in interpersonal conflicts. Just remember that two people can interpret the same event very differently. Obvious, yes. But the truth is this fact underlies much of the anger we experience because different explanations of the same event are a major source of conflict.

For example, you think the missed deadline is due to a last-minute change in strategy; your boss attributes the missed deadline to your inefficiency. Both of these perceptions will cause you and your boss to act differently. Each of you will defend your position. Conflict is inevitable. Anger is created and the situation is compounded because the angrier you become, the more rigid your thinking becomes. Consequently, you are stuck in your position, making it impossible for you to consider alternative explanations, let alone listen to an opposing view.

The antidote is simple: Remember the tip that in an anger-provoking situation, you are to immediately think of an alternative explanation, preferably how the other person may be interpreting the same situation. Here, instead of explaining the situation from your own perspective (that your boss doesn't understand the impact of a changed marketing strategy), you may find it more useful to explain the situation from your boss's perspective (that you could have handled the situation more effectively). With this explanation, your line of thinking becomes, "Gee, maybe I could have handled the project more successfully. Maybe I can learn from my boss how to do it better next time." With these thoughts, you approach your boss with concern and inquiry rather than with hostility and accusations. Only by looking at alternative views will you be able to decide which perception holds the most truth. While the accurate appraisal may still instigate anger, at least conflict due to differing perceptions is minimized, putting you and your adversary in a better place for resolution.

Research also indicates that generating alternative explanations for yourself and others is a very effective way of changing the anger mood—the thoughts, feelings, and emotions that surround an anger-provoking event and often linger for hours, days, and sometimes weeks. Be sure to make use of this fact.

The next time, for example, you note a fellow worker responding with anger over increasing budget restraints, point out something along the lines that it is not a personal vendetta but a business decision based on company performance. Or simply ask her, "Under the circumstances, what would you prefer the company to do?" I have found that such responses not only reduce anger because they put the event in proper perspective, but also often generate problem-solving behaviors that may prevent the anger-provoking situation from recurring. At the very least, you help the individual begin the process of managing his anger.

Two crucial points to note. First, the alternative explanation you give yourself and/or to another must be believable. If it isn't, it will quickly be dismissed and anger will return unchecked.

Second, speed of intervention is essential. The longer you wait to produce an alternative explanation, the less likely you will be able to generate one; your thinking will already be too rigidified, making it hard to consider alternative viewpoints. This is often the case when a person has been angry for a while and no matter what you say, she doesn't want to hear it. The key is to give the explanations early in the anger-arousing process. Again, this highlights the importance of self-awareness: The faster you know you are becoming angry, the faster you can intervene and explain the anger away.

Generating alternative explanations is a powerful anger management tool because it is easy to use and can be applied in a wide variety of daily situations. As an exercise, think of recent anger-provoking situations. Develop alternative explanations and see how they affect your anger.

The astute reader realizes that generating alternative explanations is a technique for making cognitive appraisal work for her.

Combating Anger Distortions

Recall that much of your anger is created and perpetuated by distorted thinking styles and the self-statements they produce. Because distorted thinking styles are so prevalent and powerful, you need to be able to effectively combat them. You need to counterpunch.

Like the boxer who must counterpunch his opponent to neutralize him, so you too must counterpunch the mental punches you inflict upon yourself; otherwise, you become senseless. Here, your counterpunches will take the form of a rational comeback— self-statements that help you put the provoking event in perspective.

To do this, you must be able to use your anger as a cue that it is time to reexamine your thinking. Specifically, as soon as you begin to feel angry or when you are angry, ask yourself the question: What am I telling myself about this situation? Your answer will make you aware of the self-statements you are using and what distorted thinking might be operating. If a distorted thinking style is absent, your anger is probably justified.

Note how self-awareness is essential. If you fail to recognize when you are becoming angry, or even if you are angry, your thinking will continue along the same route. Therefore, the sooner you recognize your anger, the sooner you can start to counterpunch.

The prerequisite to being an effective counterpuncher is being familiar with the conceptual thinking of each cognitive distortion and the specific self-statements a particular style causes; otherwise, you will not be ready to counterpunch with a rational comeback. For example, let's take destructive labeling.

The concept for counterpunching destructive labeling is that destructive labels are inaccurate because they describe the whole picture on the basis of one or two incidents. They are based on limited cognitive information. Limit your observations to a specific case and gather as much data as you can to get a better view of the whole picture.

Next, know how the distortion would appear in action. For destructive labeling: "My boss is a real jerk." "He's so incompetent." "She's a real bitch."

Now fight back with a counterpunch. "Be specific. They are not always like this."

Go through this procedure for each of the four cognitive distorted thinking styles. It is best if you, not someone else, devise your own counterpunch statements since they will be more meaningful to you.

Also remember that your internal dialogues can take many forms when you are angry and you certainly can influence them. Of course, we lose this ability when our anger takes hold of us. Having a constant reminder of how and what you can think when you are becoming angry is very helpful. I recommend that you write down your counterpunch statements on five- by eight-inch cards and put them in places that will remind you that you have options on how you can speak to yourself when you are angry. These visual reminders will increase the likelihood that you use counterpunching. Computers, phones, the refrigerator, and the night table are all good locations to put these helpful self-statements.

A final note for counterpunching. Your anger distortions have been winning for years. People who are good counterpunchers have excellent staying power. They do not counterpunch just once or twice; they keep punching until they knock the anger distortions out of their minds. This is the trick to counterpunching—you must keep it up. Think of yourself as Rocky and go the distance against the anger distortions. Eventually, they will disappear and you will be left with productive ways of appraising a situation.

Anger Management Instructions

Many times you will be angry and there will be no anger distortions. Your anger is valid and just. There will also be many times when you know you will soon be confronting a situation that could be anger arousing, like a difficult customer or some disgruntled union workers. In these instances, you can cognitively manage your anger by using your self-statements as self-instructions—specific statements that tell you what to do when you are getting angry or about to confront a provocation. Here are some examples of effective anger management instructions that you may use but, again, it is best to develop your own:

I can work out a plan to handle this.
Remember, stick to the issues and don't take it personally.
Don't yell.
Take a deep breath.
Listen to what they say.

Using self-statements as instructions is effective because they control your anger arousal, guide your behavior in a productive direction, prevent you from getting sidetracked, and give you confidence that you can cope with the provocation.

Clarifying Expectations

One of the most common cognitive processes we use daily is foresight—anticipating what events we are going to encounter. Although it is impossible to predict the future, there is no doubt that those who can accurately "anticipate" the future put themselves in a better position to deal with upcoming events and, at the same time, prevent themselves from becoming angry about what they thought was or wasn't going to happen.

In our daily activities, foresight comes into play under the concept of expectations—mental bets we make with ourselves about the outcome of future events, our behavior, and the behavior of others. Our expectations often reflect our goals and standards.

When expectations are miscommunicated, unrealistic, or unmet, frequent responses are frustration, anger, and, in many cases, depression. It is not surprising, therefore, that clarifying expectations is an effective anger management intervention.

My years as an angerologist have given me a modus operandi I want to pass on to you.

The first step is to identify your expectations. I suggest you write down what you expect from yourself, your boss, co-workers, and other significant people in your work life. This may seem laborious, but once you write down your expectations, you will be able to appraise them more accurately. I have found that there are several ways to tune in to the reality of your expectations.

One is to use similar past experiences as your baseline. If you expect your business or income to increase by 30 percent over the next year, but past experience shows the best you've ever done is a 20 percent increase, you are probably setting yourself up for disappointment (realistically, a 15 percent increase would be terrific and 10 percent would still be great). If you are expecting a client to triple his order, you'd best remember that the past shows he talks it up big but orders small. By using past experiences as your database, you have a valid method for forming realistic expectations.

It is good policy to ask others what they think. Sometimes it's difficult to be honest with yourself. Sharing expectations you have of yourself with other people gives you input as to whether or not you are being too hard (or easy) on yourself. They can help you evaluate expectations in terms of realism.

A third method to assess whether your expectations are realistic is to assign percentages to your expected outcomes. Quantifying the chances for your "expected" raise (60 percent chance, 50 percent chance, 20 percent chance) helps you think clearly as to whether you really believe the expectation is going to be met. Once you assign a percentage to your expectation, you can modify it as the situation evolves and, in the process, develop a realistic outlook. This illustrates an important point: Expectations will serve you best when they are elastic rather than static.

The second step toward clarifying expectations—when others are involved—is to communicate those expectations. Letting people know what is hoped for gives them the opportunity to determine if your expectation is realistic; that is, if they believe they can meet it. If they think they can't, they are able to explain their viewpoint, and together you can reach a realistic expectation. Letting people know what you expect of them also provides them with important information—what you think and what your needs are.

Mental Rehearsal

One of the more unique cognitive processes of humans is the ability to conjure up and visualize themselves in almost any situation while sitting in their living rooms. Sometimes referred to as the "imagining process," this important cognitive faculty can facilitate your ability to manage anger when you use it in the context of mental rehearsal, an intervention that incorporates many of the other cognitive interventions already cited.

Mental rehearsal is based on two well-validated assumptions. The first is that imagining can evoke the same response as an individual makes in reality. Consider the research by physiologist Edmund Jacobson, who has shown that when a person vividly imagines running, there are small but measurable contractions in his muscles comparable to the changes that occur during actual running. Similarly, by holding a rich, provoking image in your mind you can raise your blood pressure, accelerate your pulse and perspiration rate, and elicit dryness of the mouth.

The second assumption is that one of the most effective ways to learn a new behavior is to observe and imitate someone else doing it successfully. A shy salesman can watch his co-worker initiate a conversation and imitate the "model."

Mental rehearsal relies upon a most basic type of learning: creating and patterning ourselves after the perfect and rich images we envision. By identifying, refining, and practicing in our minds the steps necessary for successfully confronting a provocation, it becomes easier to face that provocation in real life. In short, we model the behavior we have already carried out in our minds.

A good way to use mental rehearsal is to arrange your provocations in order of the severity of your response. Relax in a comfortable setting and visualize yourself confronting each provocation. Be sure your practices include using your anger management instructions and hearing yourself counterpunching. The procedure usually takes fifteen to twenty minutes per provocation.

Key Concepts: Anger and thinking affect each other, and by learning to manage your thinking, you can control the anger experiences you encounter. Of particular importance is the fact that when you become angry, your thinking becomes rigid and you are, therefore, prevented from accurately appraising a situation and generating the best response. Cognitive anger management interventions allow you to counteract the effects of this mental rigidity by helping you, in a variety of ways, keep your mental flexibility, a key attribute of the successful anger manager.

Anger and
Emotions

Emotions and moods are universal and whether you are a human or a dog you have them. I have spent a great deal of time studying the subject of emotions and moods in both humans and animals, and I think the first point that should be made is that emotions perform three crucial functions in our lives.

First, emotions and moods provide us with important information about ourselves and others. Anger, for example, alerts us that something is wrong; enthusiasm tells us there's excitement. What I call working depression—complaining about your job, a negative attitude toward the company, bad-mouthing of everybody and everything—communicates helplessness and dissatisfaction. Becoming sensitive to "emotion information" gives you a significant edge by increasing your awareness of what others around you are experiencing as well as a greater understanding of yourself.

Second, emotions arouse us. In the case of anger, it can potentiate a feeling of control. Emotional arousal in itself is extremely powerful, so it is necessary to know not only how to manage it, but also how to stir it up in others in the form of motivation and enthusiasm.

Third, emotions help us communicate information to others. When you get angry, that anger signals, overtly or subconsciously, to others that something is bothering you. Indeed, this is the main purpose of emotions in animals—to let others know what you are experiencing and what you are apt to do.

By managing the emotional dimension of anger, you will be able to get emotions, anger specifically, to work for you. I think this has great significance because the role of emotions in the context of work is becoming more and more acknowledged to be an important aspect of productivity.

The Emotional Side of Anger

Anger and emotions go hand in hand. After all, anger is an emotion, and who could possibly deny that when you are angry, especially having an outburst, you are emotional.

Much can be said about the emotional aspect of anger. I believe, as an angerologist, two areas will help you the most.

The first is managing the physical arousal that accompanies anger so that you can be cool, calm, and collected in the most heated of situations, thereby increasing your chances of generating the best response to the provoking event. Being unable to do this will result in your anger getting the best of you and, more often than you think, lead to serious career setbacks.

The second area focuses on a contemporary groundbreaking area of research and application—emotional contagion: how emotions—particularly anger—spread from one person to another and how emotional contagion can be used to your advantage. For example, spreading enthusiasm throughout an organization or preventing yourself from "catching" your boss's anger.

What Do We Mean by Emotions?

A good place to start is to have some clarification of what exactly we are talking about when we use the term *emotions*, a subject that has been studied for hundreds of years.

Although there are many theories of emotions and different definitions of what they are, the most accepted thinking today suggests that emotions are best thought of as a complex composition of many components. These include subjective feelings; action tendencies (behaviors); appraisals; facial, vocal, and postural expressions; and physiological processes. While early theorists focused on the "sequence" question—which comes first, the cognitive, somatovisceral, and behavioral aspects of emotion— recent theorists conclude that "it depends." Emotional stimuli may well trigger the conscious, somatovisceral, and behavioral aspects of emotion almost simultaneously. Which appears first depends on the person and the situation. In any case, the brain integrates the emotional information it receives; each of the emotional components acts on and is in turn acted upon by the other; thus, all components are important in shaping an emotional experience.

We will put our attention here on what I believe is the crual component in the process of managing the emotional dimension of anger—physical arousal. When you are angry, this physical arousal, when unchecked, becomes anger arousal and is a major factor in causing your demise.

Emotional anger management interventions are designed to master the physiological arousal that accompanies the emotional experience of anger and prevent that arousal from becoming anger arousal. The end result is that you are able to keep your emotions from getting out of control and, at the same time, convert the physical arousal into a powerful source of energy that helps you productively manage the provocation.

THE PHYSIOLOGY OF ANGER

There can be no doubt that anger arousal is bad for you, and this is why it is so important to be able to manage it. While I am most concerned with the how-tos of anger management, I think you should know a little about the physiology of anger so that you can see for yourself why it is imperative that you manage anger arousal.

Each year, more and more studies indicate that mismanaged anger significantly contributes to a host of physical ailments. These include cardiovascular disease, digestive disorders, hypertension, headaches, rashes, and susceptibility to infections.

Here is a brief explanation of how this occurs: Repeated bouts of anger elevate levels of testosterone (for men), cortisol, epinephrine, and norepinephrine. Chronic high levels of cortisol and testosterone increase the likelihood of atherosclerosis, the most common cause of coronary artery disease. High levels of cortisol also depress the immune system, reducing the body's ability to battle infection.

Norepinephrine and epinephrine stimulate the sympathetic nervous system to shunt blood from the skin, liver, and digestive tract to the heart, lungs, and skeletal muscles. Blood pressure becomes elevated and glucose is dumped into the blood system to provide energy for confrontation or escape. However, when blood is shunted away from the liver, the liver loses its efficiency for clearing the blood of cholesterol, contributing to the buildup of fatty deposits in the arteries. High blood pressure also weakens the heart by making it work harder, resulting in a large and less efficient heart muscle. Arteries are also damaged by the high pressure of blood flow. The artery wall develops tiny tears, which fatty deposits cover. These deposits can grow to fill the artery and may eventually stop the flow of blood.

One recent significant finding is that some angry people of both sexes have an underactive parasympathetic nervous system that fails to produce the common hormone acetylcholine, which normally turns off the harsh effects of adrenaline produced by the sympathetic nervous system when you are angry. Over time, too much adrenaline and too little acetylcholine can lead to a host of problems. The arteries grow stiffer from constantly elevated blood pressure and the heart weakens from being overexerted. The stress hormones previously mentioned get out of control and create adverse effects. Thus, managing anger arousal is particularly important to the individual who finds himself getting angry several times a day or who stays angry for extended durations— staying angry after a three o'clock meeting until dinnertime would qualify as an extended duration.

EMOTIONAL ANGER MANAGEMENT INTERVENTIONS

Emotional anger management interventions share the common denominator of utilizing the physical arousal that accompanies anger to your advantage. (In contrast, many of the cognitive interventions use your thinking as a cue that you are becoming angry.) This can be accomplished in three ways.

First, by learning how to use the arousal as a signal that it is time for you to respond differently, in a way that keeps the physical arousal from becoming anger arousal.

Second, by generating a different type of physical arousal that is antagonistic to anger arousal.

And third, by learning how to convert the physical arousal into a form of energy that gives you the impetus to confront your provocations effectively.

My experience has found that there are three interventions that can help you manage the arousal aspect of anger, and perhaps other emotions too. These interventions are:

Body Biofeedback
Generating Alternative Arousals
Channeling Arousal

Body Biofeedback

If you are not familiar with the concept of biofeedback, it is the process of altering your physiological responses by consciously controlling the information received about how your body is currently responding. Hundreds of studies have shown that people provided with this information are able to lower their blood pressure, slow down or increase their heartbeat, and control their perspiration rate as well as influence many other physiological mechanisms.

Body biofeedback adapts the preceding principle: By learning how your body feels when it is on the verge of experiencing anger arousal, you can use that feeling as a cue for altering your physiological responses or modifying your thoughts and behavior so that your anger arousal does not get out of control. The faster you can recognize that your body is becoming angry, the faster you can respond.

Therefore, you must learn what your body feels like when it is on the verge of anger arousal. The steps to take are recognizing when you are physically tense and learning to be sensitive to different levels of physiological arousal.

THE IMPORTANCE OF TENSION

Tension is the initial stage in anger arousal. When we feel strung out, we are more easily provoked. Tense muscles, headaches, and tightness in the chest reduce our tolerance to cope effectively with daily provocations. If our tension level is high, we may treat a minor annoyance as though it were a catastrophe, with resultant waste of energy. Recognizing tension as a cue that anger may be brewing is essential because you can then respond differently, and thereby stop a potential outburst of destructive anger from occurring.

We all experience tension physically when we stay in the same position too long. Muscles benefit from movement and need the circulation of blood that movement produces. Movement directly induces relaxation because muscles work in pairs, one group relaxing as the opposing group contracts. Bend your arm at the elbow and you'll get the point.

When muscles are tight and in static contraction for long periods, the circulation is impeded and there will be a buildup of fatigue, which may lead to muscle spasms (cramps). Holding a fist clenched for a while can significantly raise your blood pressure, and most dentists will warn you that continual tension of the jaw with teeth clenched tightly together is a common cause of tension headaches as well as of dental disorders. These are only some of the effects of sustained muscle tension.

Often our body biofeedback tells us it's tense and we don't listen. Has your foot ever "fallen asleep"? Have you ever risen from a chair and noted soreness in your spine? And right now, some of you may be experiencing tension reading this book. Your shoulders may be still, legs cramped, and jaws clenched, causing fatigue and interfering with your ability to concentrate.

Intermittently, mild tension is not harmful, but prolonged tension does damage, wearing us out and draining physical and psychological resources we need to deal effectively with daily provocations.

In order to hear your body say it's tense, you have to be aware of what it feels like in that condition. Over the years, I have found the quickest and most effective way to do this is by consciously experiencing the difference between two polar states, tension and relaxation.

The procedure I recommend has you tighten and relax different muscle groups in your body. By practicing the method several times, you will begin to gain greater awareness as to when you are experiencing physical tension. You can then respond by breaking the tension in one of several easy ways that give immediate results.

- Try a ten-second massage. Whether it's a stiff neck, a stiff shoulder, or a headache, ten seconds of rubbing will reduce tension and make you feel better.
- You may change your posture. If you're sitting or standing, changing the position of your body will break the lock. This is great for when you are on your way to an important meeting and are stuck in traffic or sitting at your desk doing a major task.
- You can reach out. Extending your arms and legs gets the kinks out and the circulation moving.
- Give yourself a wink. Close your eyes for less than a minute and shut out the pressure. When you open your eyes, you may see things differently.

In essence, know when you are tense so you can prevent yourself from making the situation, let alone your health, worse.

DISCRIMINATING AROUSALS

If you ignore your body when it tells you it is tense, chances are it will soon yell at you because it wants you to know that something is wrong. It's hard to believe, but even when most peoples' bodies are yelling at them, they still don't listen. Even when your body is breathing hard, perspiring, and jacking up its blood pressure, you ignore it. Your heart is now at risk. If you think this doesn't happen to you, think again. Remember the last time you were in a heated argument with a team member. Despite the fact your body was yelling at you, you probably continued arguing or being very upset.

To know when your body is experiencing anger arousal, develop a sensitivity to your different levels of physical arousal, paying particular attention to those bodily or somatic functions that are disturbed when your body experiences anger. These include your heart rate, perspiration rate, respiration rate, and muscular tension. They also include any other changes that are unique to you, such as dry mouth, loud voice, or headaches. All these somatic functions are different when you are physically aroused, not aroused at all, or anger aroused. The better you become at noticing the differences among these physical states, the faster you can use anger arousal as a cue that your body is yelling at you.

Develop this discriminating ability by identifying three distinct times: When you feel relaxed, when you are in a rush or doing any activity that requires your body to work, and when you are angry. Observe your physical reactions and you will note the obvious: that the difference in your heart rate and breathing rate dramatically increase as you move from a resting state to an angry state. Because these differences are so noticeable and because you are increasing your sensitivity to them, your general ability to note slight shifts in your arousal will become common practice in about a week. You will become more aware of when you are getting angry because you will be more sensitive and aware of anger arousal feelings.

What if you fail to recognize the buildup of anger arousal? By definition, of course, you will then be very angry. But you can still take steps to manage the anger arousal. The generic strategy is to slow yourself down. Try these actions:

- Speak more slowly.
- Get yourself a drink of water. This will literally help you cool off. Drinks with caffeine may stimulate the fight-or-flight response and increase the arousal you want to slow down.
- If you are sitting down, lean back. When you're yelling, leaning forward is part of the fighting posture.
- Keep your hands at your sides. Shaking your fists and waving your arms speeds up your circulation.
- Quiet yourself. Sometimes do everyone a favor by telling yourself to shut up.

Generating Alternative Arousals

A second category of emotional anger management interventions is based on the strategy of using anger as a cue to generate an alternative type of physical arousal that is antagonistic to anger arousal. This has the effect of dissipating anger arousal or at least reducing it to a more manageable state. There are two types of arousal that fit this bill. One is generated through relaxation; the other through humor.

RELAXATION

Humans react in a predictable way to acute and chronic stressful situations that trigger the inborn part of our physiological makeup called the fight-or-flight response. When we encounter situations that challenge our survival, the fight-flight response increases our blood pressure, heart rate, rate of respiration, blood flow to the muscles, and metabolism, all of which prepare us for either direct conflict or escape. However, the fight-flight response is frequently not used as intended; that is, in preparation for running or for fighting with an enemy, a survival mechanism. It is often brought on by situations that require us to make behavioral adjustments— a new job, loss of a job, death of a loved one, divorce, marriage, change of financial status. When the fight-flight response is invoked inappropriately and repeatedly, it can lead to disturbed health.

Anger as an emotion is a derivative of the fight-flight response. This is why people who experience frequent and intense outbursts of the emotion are prone to adverse physical conditions. They are using the fight-flight response inappropriately. By generating a physiological response of relaxation, you decrease sympathetic nervous system activity and restore your body to its normal balance. To produce "when-needed relaxation," develop a conditioned relaxation response (CRR). In contrast to practicing relaxation for the sake of relaxation (this is in fact good for you), the idea here is to use relaxation as an intervention—an optional way of responding—in anger-arousing situations.

The intervention's underlying concept is associative learning. Here you will be "associating" a physiological state (relaxation) with specific images and thoughts. By practicing the association, your thoughts (remember the cognitive section) will develop the power to evoke the physiological state of relaxation. Given an anger-provoking event or knowing that you will soon be encountering a difficult situation, you will be able to evoke your conditioned relaxation response, thus allowing you to keep your physical arousal from becoming anger arousal. You act more productively.

There are numerous techniques you can use to develop your relaxation response, such as Transcendental Meditation, Zen, yoga, progressive relaxation, self-hypnosis, autogenic training, and biofeedback. There are four essential components that irrespective of method are thought to be necessary to develop a relaxation response.

- A quiet environment. When developing your CRR, choose a quiet, calm environment without distractions. This will make it easier to avoid interfering stimuli when you are focusing on your relaxing images and/or statements.
- A cognitive device. Having a cognitive device—a sound, word, image, statement, fixed gaze—helps you shift your mind from being externally oriented to being internally oriented. This is important because it enables you to "feel" what is going on in your body. Having a constant word or image also helps you overcome a major obstacle in developing your CRR: mind wandering. Saying the word "breaks" your distracting thoughts. Use the same image, word, sound, or other cognitive device each time you practice your relaxing procedure. This consistency will increase the power of your cognitive device to elicit the desired level of physiological arousal.

- A passive attitude. Passivity is probably the most important component in developing your CRR. Distracting thoughts will occur. Do not worry when this happens; just return to your cognitive device. If you worry about how well you are doing, you may prevent the CRR from happening. Adapt a "let it happen" attitude. Distracting thoughts do not mean you are doing something incorrectly. They are to be expected.
- A comfortable position. When you practice your CRR, it is important to be in a comfortable position so that there is no undue muscular tension. If a position gets uncomfortable, it is a signal that tension is increasing. So switch to a position that makes you feel more at ease.

I have found that most people can develop a CRR in ten to fourteen days if they practice twenty minutes a day.

Your relaxation response will come in handy. You can use it at the first signs of feeling tense and irritable, thereby preventing full-blown anger from developing. Use it when someone expresses anger at you. Here it will prevent you from escalating the situation and allow you to listen to your boss, for example, without being defensive. Many times, if he sees you "relaxed" and paying attention, he is more likely to calm down too. It's also helpful when you know you are going to have to confront an anger-arousing situation. Your CRR will help you stay in control and appraise the situation accurately. In fact, most people who use their CRR before they encounter the provocation report much greater success in confronting it than their counterparts.

HUMOR

A female manager told me that every time her boss got angry at her, he would go into an emotional tirade of abusive name calling. After many of these terrible experiences, the heroine prepared a three-by-five-inch card that listed all of her boss's favorite nicknames which he used when he was angry. She kept it handy. At the inevitable outburst, she whipped out the card and, giving it to him, proclaimed, "Here, boss. I made it easy for you. Just go down the list." A second of shock turned into moments of laughter and the situation never occurred again.

This is just one of many examples that show a good sense of humor is a valuable job skill. Here I refer to sense of humor as not only being able to laugh, especially at yourself, but, equally important, knowing *when* to use humor, "sensing" that it is a good response.

Humor, more specifically laughter, creates a physiological arousal that is antagonistic to anger arousal. When you laugh, you release the physical (and mental) tension that is leading you toward anger arousal. On a more scientific note, laughter stimulates the release of endorphins (any of a group of proteins). As the level of endorphins in the brain *increases*, the perception of pain *decreases*. In effect, laughter causes our bodies to produce our own painkiller. It reduces some of the "pain" that anger brings and is an effective anger management intervention.

Besides the benefit of laughing arousal, you are helped another way too. For at least a moment, you can forget about your troubles. But that brief moment gives you the time to reappraise the situation more accurately, and in a better mood.

You can increase your laughter by developing your sense of humor. Speaking for myself, I recommend the following:

- Put on your *Candid Camera* glasses. Take ten minutes or so out of your day, distance yourself from your job and home, and pretend it's a *Candid Camera* episode and you're the camera. Look around you, observe all the silly, goofy, and therefore very human activities going on that just ten minutes before seemed so damn serious, earthshaking, and stomach churning. This can be a terrifically lightening and enlightening experience.
- Humor meditation. For five or ten minutes or whatever

amount of time you can spare during the tensest part of your day, stop to take a humor-meditation break. During this meditation, shut out the world and read a funny passage from a joke book or from a humor scrapbook or think of a past funny experience.

- Create a humor-filled environment by setting up a bulletin board in your room or office that has cartoons, funny photographs, jokes, and humorous quotes on it.
- Start to anticipate situations in which you could use a humor response—staff meetings, performance appraisals, dealing with customers. I think you will find that by thinking about these situations, you will develop a better sense of when humor can be productive.

Your ongoing assignment is to have fifteen laughs a day. Three should be belly laughs.

Channeling Arousal

Channeling arousal is the culminating emotional anger management intervention. It refers to the ability to convert your anger arousal into a powerful source of energy that helps you handle a provocation productively. In essence, you are taking advantage of the fact that your body is raring to go. What it needs is direction; the arousal becomes focused. You are energizing yourself.

Channel your arousal by using it as a cue to say, "What is the best thing for me to do?" Your answer gives you guidance and you will have the energy to act.

For example, if you have just made a disappointing presentation that evokes your anger and maybe that of your boss, your best bet is to immediately say, "What's the best thing to do?" Your answer is apt to help you focus on making your next presentation stellar rather than on abusing your assistant or getting an ulcer.

What should be immediately apparent is the importance of speed of responding. If you channel the arousal quickly, you will have the physical arousal to convert into feelings of motivation. If, however, you wait too long before channeling, it will become intense anger arousal, which will get the better of you, or will diminish to the point that you do nothing to resolve the provocation and the pattern is sure to repeat.

What Is Emotional Contagion?

A co-worker shouts at you.
You shout back.

This is an example of emotional contagion, a powerful process that will help you manage anger and improve the functioning of your organization and the members who comprise it.

In the last year or two, researchers have found that many emotions—anger, fear, sadness, anxiety, and enthusiasm—are like social viruses: They literally can spread from one individual to another, whether it's at home or in the office. The pop phrase is "contagious emotions."

More specifically, emotional contagion may be defined as the tendency to "catch" (experience/express) another person's emotions—his or her emotional appraisals, subjective feelings, expressions, patterned physiological processes (e.g., breathing rate, eye contact, gestures), and behavior. The common occurrence of one person's shouting triggering another's is a good example of the process in action.

Emotional contagion is important because it provides a fresh perspective about emotions and moods in organizational life. It would be hard to refute that most of the working world shies away from emotions, moods, and feelings because conventional wisdom says these factors have little to do with business. In fact, most of the time, emotions and moods are thought to get the way of making sound business decisions.

Rather than projecting the feeling that emotions and moods are inappropriate to the business world and that to express these human urges is a sign of weakness, emotional contagion tells us that emotions provide important information about an individual. By being sensitive to this information, you can conduct yourself much more effectively. Emotional contagion tells us that emotions can no longer be thought of as insignificant factors or out of place when it comes to doing business. Quite the contrary: Emotions can be powerful tools that strongly influence productivity and improve our interpersonal effectiveness. Here is an example of an individual who makes emotional contagion work for her:

An administrative assistant talks casually with her boss. Suddenly, she notices that she is beginning to feel awkward, uncomfortable, and ill at ease. She worries that she must be boring her boss and tries harder to be interesting. The intensity of the discomfort grows, so she apologetically bids her boss farewell. As she walks away feeling somewhat anxious, she recalls that she was feeling fine prior to speaking with her boss. She wonders if she could possibly have picked up her boss's emotion. She realizes that her boss is always ill at ease in company: Brief expressions of anxiety cross her face, her voice rises, she gets "twitchy." The next time they meet, the assistant worries less about being interesting and more about reassuring her anxious boss. That succeeds in putting them both at ease.

Another reason to study emotional contagion's relevance to the working world is that it gives us a mechanism for stopping the flow of negative emotions that all too often permeate today's organizations. Anger, depression, anxiety—in the guise of low morale—stunt organizational effectiveness if not contained and managed effectively. Indeed, one of the most frequent questions asked by seminar participants is "How do you handle the person who is always negative, always complaining?" Further exploration reveals that "negative persons" are difficult to deal with because "they bring everyone else down." Emotional contagion is the process that allows the negative person to depress those around him, but it is also the process we can use to immunize ourselves from catching negative emotions.

Finally, emotional contagion is important because it shows us how we can transfer positive emotions to others. Certainly, the sales manager who can "mood infect" his staff with a shot of enthusiasm has an edge over his counterpart. Psychologists, students of organizational behavior, and corporations have long searched for ways to energize their constituencies. In this context, emotional contagion is a crucial component of motivating others.

To take advantage of emotional contagion, we must examine the process in more detail. Specifically, we must first examine the theoretical underpinning of how people catch another's emotions. Then we can get to our main concern, which is how to make emotional contagion work for us.

THE SPREADING OF EMOTIONS

Individuals "catch" each other's emotions in several ways. Early researchers focused on complex cognitive processes by which people might come to know and feel what those around them felt. Some theorists proposed that conscious reasoning and analysis accounted for emotional contagion. For example, as subjects (sales reps) listen to a target (customer) describe his or her emotional experiences, they might remember times they felt much the same way and shared much the same experiences. Such conscious reveries could spark a similar emotional response.

Other researchers argued that emotional contagion was a conditioned emotional response. If, for example, an upset boss lashes out at his subordinate, then soon the sight of a distressed boss will elicit distress in the subordinate. Through stimulus generalization (responding similarly to similar events), emotional contagion could result from the sight of distress in *anyone*, not just the boss.

A few researchers have suggested that some forms of emotional contagion are the result of even more primitive associative processes; specifically, that on occasion people may catch each other's emotions because some actions or feelings generate an unconditioned emotional response. For example, abrupt, angular movements; shrill, high-pitched voices; and loud or otherwise intense vocalizations or movements probably elicit emotional responses. Although individuals might be aware of their emotional response, they might be utterly ignorant of the stimulus to which they're reacting and, therefore, powerless against the emotional forces automatically unleashed following the perception of the stimulus.

Finally, and most important, is the fact that people continually mimic and synchronize their movements with the facial expressions, voices, postures, and behaviors of others.

If we piece together several facts about the nature of emotions, we can gain some understanding of how and when each of these mechanisms might operate, and thus begin to make them work for us.

Emotional Information May Be Processed Consciously or Unconsciously

People often have powerful emotional reactions to others, yet are at a loss to explain just why they responded as they did. Lots of thinking goes on at "low frequency," if you will, an almost subconscious level. Neuroscientists have found that people are consciously aware of only a small bit of the information that their brains process moment to moment. Normally, people consciously attend to only the most important, unusual, or difficult information. Indeed, it is the exception, not the rule, when thinking is conscious; by its very nature, conscious thought seems the only sort of thinking we do. Emotional contagion seems to be produced by information that is processed outside of conscious awareness.

Despite the fact that information is processed sequentially, the human brain is clearly capable of processing information in parallel. For example, while we are carrying on a rational conversation, we may also be continually monitoring our partner's emotional reactions to what we have to say. We may unconsciously and automatically scan our partner's face for second-by-second information as to his or her feelings. Is he or she feeling happiness, love, anger, sadness, or fear? We can use a variety of subtle indicators (such clues as facial muscle movements, microexpressions, crooked expressions, or the timing of reactions) to decide if the other person is telling the truth or lying. People may even be able to detect their partner's mood by observing facial muscle movements so minute that they seem detectable only in electromyographic recordings. People may also respond to other types of emotional information. They can listen to other people's words—to the volume, rhythm, pitch, and rapidity of their speech or to the length of their pauses. They can observe the way people gesture, move their legs and feet, and stand. They can observe other's behaviors.

Given this view of emotion, there is really not much mystery about the observations of therapists or others that although they are not consciously aware that their clients and others are experiencing joy, sadness, fear, or anger that "somehow" they sense what others are feeling and react to it. Today, emotion researchers assume that the information we are consciously aware of is only a small portion of the knowledge we possess about ourselves and others.

People Mimic or Synchronize Their Movements with Those of People Around Them

There is no particular need for people to be consciously aware that they are synchronizing their actions with those of others. Any action that is performed continually is likely to become automatic. Nonetheless, the ability to be in tune with those around us is critically important. It allows us to coordinate emotionally and physically with them. There is evidence that people synchronize their facial muscle movements, voices, and postural movements with one another and, therefore, tend to be in emotional synchrony. These are the main mechanisms of emotional contagion, and thus the evidence for their emotional transmission power should be highlighted.

Facial Mimicry It has been observed that when babies open their mouths, mothers tend to open theirs too. This is a nondeliberate reaction on their part and one of which the mothers can be completely unaware. It has also been found that people imitate others' expressions of pain, laughter, smiling, anger, affection, embarrassment, discomfort, disgust, stuttering, reaching with effort, and the like in a broad range of situations.

In essence, the perception of another face is not just an information transfer but a very literal means by which we feel the sensations that the other feels. Perhaps this is the reason why smiling faces at parties or grief at a time of mourning are infectious.

Vocal Synchrony It has been speculated that people's speech rhythms are related to their biological rhythms. Different people, therefore, prefer different interaction tempos at different periods. When partners interact, if things are to go well, their speech cycles must become mutually entrained. Consistent with this reasoning, there is a good deal of evidence (for example, from controlled interview settings) supporting patterns between speakers, speech rate, pauses, and response lags. There is also clear evidence that over time, partners come to match one another's conversational rhythms, even in moment-to-moment reactions. People also match one another's rhythms as measured by length of vocalizations, mean pause duration, time between turns, length of talkovers, and the probability of interrupting. Note the next time someone is arguing with you and observe whether or not you are yelling back with the same pace and intensity. Most likely you are.

Movement Coordination Finally, communication researchers have noted that people often synchronize their rhythms and movements with those of the person with whom they are interacting. A speaker's speech and movements are mirrored in the listeners' flow of movements. When the speaker is talking and moving, the listener is moving as well. A typical research analysis of this is as follows:

When B is moving, his movements are coordinated with T's movements and speech, and that these movements amount in part to a "mirror image" of T's movements. As T leans back in his chair, B leans back and lifts his head; then B moves his right arm to the right, just as T moves his left arm to the left, and B follows with a head cock to the right, just as T cocks his head to the left. We might say that here B dances T's dance.

Key Concepts: Emotional contagion refers to the process of how an individual's emotional state is literally transmitted to another. The dominant way in which these emotions are transferred is through mimicking another's behavior. This mimicry is usually beyond conscious awareness. What is mirrored—and what contains the emotion per se—are sounds, facial expressions, and movements. Anger could be spread through a rising voice, a piercing look, and gestures of the arm.

With the preceding pages of background, I can now give you what I have found to be effective ways of making emotional contagion work for you.

Making Emotional Contagion Work for You

The interventions I share with you come from my clinical expertise rather than academic studies (the subject is much too new for any studies to have been done in this particular area). Nevertheless, as an angerologist, I have experienced their success in a wide range of situations and have also heard my clinical colleagues testify to their effectiveness. I am quite confident that the following four guidelines will help you take advantage of the emotional contagion process.

1. **Immunize yourself.** Just as you immunize yourself against chicken pox, so you must do the same when dealing with contagious emotions; otherwise, you will increase your susceptibility to catching them. There are several ways to immunize yourself, all serving the purpose of helping you keep your psychological distance—not in a detached or aloof manner but in a way that allows you to either maintain the emotional state you had prior to the encounter or manage your emotional state during the encounter.

   If you are unable to keep your psychological distance, you become victimized by the other's emotional state, which frequently will be anger, depression, anxiety, and, in many organizations, fear.

   Here are three strong immunizations I suggest you take:

- Anticipate. When you know you are going to meet with someone, anticipate his emotional well-being. Do you think he will be enthused, apathetic, angry, down, or depressed? By anticipating, you will be able to work out in advance strategies for dealing with different emotional states. Do this the next time you are giving a performance appraisal or making a sales call.
- Practice relaxation. A relaxation response is an effective immunization for emotional contagion because it helps keep your emotional arousal from becoming unmanageable, which often happens when you are the target of another's anger or in the presence of an anxious person. When you are relaxed, you can assess the situation for yourself and

differentiate your own appraisals from those around you. This is especially important with anger, depression, fear, and anxiety, which are intensified by cognitive distortions.

Also, by being relaxed, you are able to stay in and manage the encounter for a longer period of time, thereby increasing the likelihood of directing it to a successful outcome.

• Use instructional self-statements. "Just because he's angry doesn't mean I have to get angry." "No matter how anxious he becomes, I will remain calm. I'll breathe deeply and speak a little slower than usual." These self-statements are powerful immunization shots because they increase your cognitive awareness of what the other individual is experiencing and guide you on how best to respond. Consequently, you are minimizing your chances of subconsciously mimicking the behaviors—and thought—that transmit contagious emotions. Take action by writing down several instructional self-statements you would use for the different emotional states you often encounter.

To be sure, there will be many times when you won't desire to influence the moods or emotions of others. But neither should you have to be affected by their emotions and moods, particularly when they are distressful. For these instances, immunizing yourself is vital simply because you will be able to cope more effectively with the emotional states of others. Anyone who lives with a chronically depressed person or who has a chronically angry boss immediately sees the value in this. At the very least, your mental and physical health improve a little.

There are also many times when you *do* want to influence the moods and emotions of others, and in these cases, being able to keep your psychological distance allows you to think strategically, to formulate options, and to decide on the spot what is the best course of action.

2. **Increase your awareness of others.** The importance of increasing your self-awareness has already been discussed. Here I want you to increase your awareness of the individual you are encountering. Remember, research shows that most of the information you process is beyond your conscious awareness.

    Increasing your awareness of others will allow you to be "on guard" to the behaviors that you typically mimic when your awareness is low. This information makes it easier to keep your psychological space; you become more adept at using the negative emotions as a cue to give yourself an immunization shot.

    With increased awareness of others, you will also be able to get a glimpse into their current emotional state. You'll begin to respond to them in a way that either intensifies the emotional state or reduces it, or you'll actually convert it to an altogether different emotional frame.

    What to do? Hear the person's voice. Note volume, speech rhythm, tone. Scan her face for frowns, scowls, and smiles. Watch her gestures and posture: arms and hands waving or hanging straight down; slumped in a chair or sitting upright; moving briskly or slowing? Paying attention to these cues is vital because each is indicative of a particular emotion or mood. True, there is not a 100 percent correlation, but a person who is speaking rapidly, changing subjects, and fidgeting briskly is probably experiencing anxiety. The person who is slumped in a chair and speaks low and slow may be depressed.

3. **Strategize.** What is the best way to cope with this person's emotional state? What are your goals? Do you need to calm down or to motivate? Perhaps empathizing is your best response.

    It has been my experience that few people strategize about how to deal with the emotional well-being of others because before they have a chance, they have already been mood-infected. This is especially true for anger, which becomes contagious almost immediately. Note that if you immunize yourself by anticipating the moods of others, you will automatically start to strategize how to respond. But you must also be able to plan on the spot, as when a subordinate suddenly becomes upset during a meeting or when a co-worker receives bad news a few minutes before your team presentation.

4. **Implement a plan.** For those times when you simply want to maintain your own emotional sanity, immunization should do the job. But if you need to influence the moods and emotions of others, you must implement a plan. The key concept here is "mood infection," which refers to the process of intentionally infecting another with a particular emotion or mood.

While we cannot go over or conceive of every situation in which you may want to influence another's emotions or moods, I have noted that there are several common situations in which mood infection skills would be valuable. Here are a few examples that show mood infection in action:

Motivating Yourself and Your Staff Have you ever had a terrible day at work, then gotten into your car, turned on the radio, and *boom!*—your favorite song came on and you began to feel great? Have you ever been at a baseball game where the hometown fans started to rhythmically clap or chant DE-FENSE, DE-FENSE, DE-FENSE and the scoreboard flashed LOUDER, LOUDER? You're clapping and yelling too. Did you see the movie *Hoosiers*? Gene Hackman plays a high school basketball coach who before each game gets his team in a huddle and has them clap until they reach a feverish pace. Then he lets them take to the court.

It may seem a bit unconventional, but you can motivate your

staff, and yourself, by mood-infecting with sound. Anger is certainly communicated by tone of voice, as is love. Remember, sound is one of the mechanisms that transfer emotions and are mimicked. Babies communicate distress to their mothers with whining and signal their contentment with cooing. Sound in itself is emotionally stimulating and specific sounds influence emotional experiences.

How you make this particular tool work for you will depend on your willingness to experiment. I would suggest, for example, that you play Coach Hackman. Get your staff together every morning for a huddle and clap until you reach a feverish pitch. It might seem silly, but the dozens of managers who have done this have told me it energizes their staffs. Many do it after lunch.

Build some upbeat music into your day. A manager told me that once a week her staff of six had to spend at least two hours doing paperwork they dreaded. It was not difficult to do, just grunt work. On one particular paperwork day, a staff member asked if anyone would mind if he turned on his portable tape deck. No one objected and so the music started. The manager noted that people seemed to enjoy it and, in fact, finished their work about twenty minutes ahead of time. The manager now has a powerful stereo in the office and swears that playing music at different parts of the day creates a more enthusiastic and productive staff.

The least effective music for motivation will be the type you hear in a dental office (note, the goal there is to calm). I find upbeat oldies usually do the trick—try early Beach Boys or Dion and the Belmonts. Again, you might find this to be hokey, but researchers have found that different types of music stimulate different emotional responses. Classical music heard for the first time, for example, has been found to evoke feelings of depression, whether the listener is American or Chinese.

Finally, use your voice strategically. Football coaches don't speak in low monotones during halftime pep talks. Nor do the effective ones rant and rave. Find the right tone by practicing out loud and noting the effect your voice has on your own physiology.

When you feel aroused, you are probably speaking in motivational sounds.

The Crucial Presentation Starting time is 10 A.M., so at 9:30, you meet with your key presenter. Paying attention to his cues, you immediately sense he is anxious.

Situations like this, ones in which you are dealing with an anxious person, happen all the time. It may be in performance appraisals, handling a first-time customer, or meeting with a new boss. Unfortunately, most of us, because of emotional contagion, pick up the anxiety of the others, which only intensifies the anxiety of the situation, making it more uncomfortable for all. Most likely, performance will be impeded.

However, if you can reduce the person's anxiety, you have the opportunity of turning the situation into a productive experience. Mood infection can help by infecting the individual with some calmness, the antithesis of anxiety. I would do it by using several components (sound, gesture, mimicry) of mood infection:

I would stay relaxed, hoping the individual might mimic my behavior. I would breathe more slowly. If sitting, I would sit relatively still. I would make sure I spoke slowly and in a soothing voice. When I did speak, I would ask open-ended questions that would serve to slow down the person's speech rhythm as well as to help her appraise her concerns more accurately. Getting rid of any cognitive distortions that are fueling her anxieties (e.g., mind reading) is the goal. Reassurance and reflective listening also help.

Co-worker Blues You share an office with a colleague, and he likes to talk to you about his problems. Needless to say, if you don't immunize yourself, not only does your work get impaired, but you can also count on going home in a bad mood every day.

Negativity bums people out. Remember, depression is a contagious mood. If it is a genuine case of clinical depression, there will be little you can do. After all, you are not a psychiatrist. Your best bet is to gently suggest that the individual seek professional help, maybe through the company medical director. However, if it's more what I refer to as working depression, then it's a different story. Mood infection may be able to help you change the person's mood to a more pleasant and productive one.

Try this: Make sure you come to work in an upbeat spirit. Have a big smile on your face—it's usually contagious. Speak in a motivational tone. Move around your space briskly.

Try to use some humor with the idea that laughing will increase your co-worker's physiological arousal—something you want to do when an individual or group is feeling down. Humor may also give him a different perspective and thus help change some of his depressing cognitive appraisals. At the same time, if appropriate, share your appraisals of the situation to which your co-worker is reacting. If you mix this with the other factors, you may succeed in getting him to catch your appraisals too.

It's obvious that the above prescription requires you to exert a tremendous amount of energy. But because depression, to say nothing of having a case of the blues, is so prevalent, and because depression is a contagious mood that will eventually drain you of your energy anyway, you may be better off to act preventively.

Defensive Subordinates A subordinate continually responds to your criticisms of his work with anger, inevitably turning every supervisory session into an ugly confrontation, with you too blowing up. In the end, being the boss, you look like the bad guy.

Whether it's a subordinate, customer, boss, or co-worker, it's a nightmare when you are the recipient of someone else's anger. Anger, more than any other emotion, is the fastest to spread and the most difficult to stop. Again, I have found that mood infection and its components can be quite helpful for these all-too-often daily encounters.

What would be your strategy? What behaviors and/or different emotions would you want to communicate? How would you do it?

If you remember that when you become angry your body—physically and mentally—is speeding up, you know that your general plan is to slow the angry person down so that he can more accurately appraise the situation and respond more productively. To use mood infection, think about what behaviors you want the individual to mimic and what type of emotional state you want him to catch. My years of experience dictate that you:

- Manage your physiological arousal: Breathe deeply and slowly.
- Sit or stand relatively still, hands at your side.
- Sit back in your chair, not on the edge leaning forward.
- Speak slowly and in a calm voice.
- Do not interrupt (you do not want him to interrupt you, which is characteristic of an angry person).
- Use humor when appropriate (will the person laugh?). Humor is antagonistic to anger arousal. You can laugh first.
- Practice any other behaviors that you think will slow the individual down and communicate a sense of calmness to him.

One point of clarification. I am not suggesting that you always want to be calm in the face of someone's anger. In some cases, this could intensify the situation and be interpreted as your not caring or seeing the significance of the situation. Indeed, one of the functions of anger is to communicate that something is wrong. The point is that the person who is angry is experiencing increased physiological arousal and that arousal must be diminished before it gets out of hand. Thus, infect with calmness by being calm, to return the physiological arousal to its homeostatic norm.

Fearful Staff Your staff is really fearful about an upcoming decision that will no doubt affect their job status and security. Trouble is no one knows when the decision is to be made, if ever, and no one knows if changes are actually going to occur. In the meantime, your staff is paralyzed by fear and productivity is hitting new lows every week. Morale stinks too.

More and more, I hear managers asking how to take care of fear in their departments. Mood infection may help.

You know you cannot act in a fearful way. Act confident, be upbeat. Again, you must slow down your behavior to avoid acting impulsively.

Show you are in control. Fear is often described as an "out-of-control state." Stick to your rituals so others will take care of business too.

Use more humor; the laughing arousal will loosen things up. Remember, emotion appraisals are contagious too.

To reiterate, the preceding mood infection interventions come from my clinical experiences, and also from distillations of research done in various areas. Certainly, questions about mood infection and emotional contagion abound, but we know the process exists. Because emotions and moods are such powerful forces in determining performance, I urge you to give the concepts serious thought and to experiment with their use. I believe the positive results you attain will put you in a better mood.

Key Concepts: Vital to making anger work for you is the ability to manage its emotional component, which generally means being able to keep the physiological arousal that accompanies anger at a moderate level so that it does not impede your thinking and behavior. Also important to remember is that many emotions, especially anger, are literally contagious and spread from one person to another through such subtle and overt responses as facial expressions, behavioral gestures, and voice patterns. By focusing on these particular responses, it is possible to keep yourself from catching another's distressful emotional state and perhaps change his emotional state to a more desirable one.

Anger and Communication

There are many episodes of anger in which you are the lone participant: getting stuck in traffic, making a poor golf shot, being unable to get your PC to do its functions. In these instances, your success in managing anger is directly related to how well you communicate with yourself (counterpunching, listening to your physical cues).

There are an equal number of times when your success in making anger work for you is a result of how well you communicate with others, either expressing your own feelings of anger or effectively listening to the anger that is directed at you. In these situations, what is needed to be a successful anger manager is being able to make communication a tool that facilitates anger resolution. Your lesson here is built around this theme.

COMMUNICATING ANGER—
INTERPERSONALLY

Over the years, the subject of anger and communication has raised many questions, but the ones I hear the most frequently center on these:

1. What is the best way to communicate anger?
2. How do you communicate or deal with an angry person or group?
3. What are the communication skills needed to manage anger so interpersonal conflict can be resolved?

Communicating Anger

It is impossible not to communicate anger when, in fact, you are angry. This is because anger is an emotion and, if you recall, a primary function of an emotion is to communicate. Therefore, anger in and of itself is a communicative mechanism; it signals that something is wrong.

There are numerous times you can probably point to in which you were angry but "didn't let the other person know it." In actuality, you might have suppressed your anger cues, making it more difficult for another to sense your mood. Do not doubt for a second, however, that you still gave off anger cues, subtle as could be. At the very least, your anger is communicated through a migraine headache or activation of an ulcer. Since you *do* communicate anger, it makes good sense to learn how to convey it effectively.

After all is said, done, and written, there are only three ways to communicate anger: Stuff it, escalate it, or, preferably, direct it.

STUFFING

Stuffing is another term for "denial." When you stuff your anger, you avoid the person or the situation that is provoking your anger. Stuffers pretend they are not upset. Here are some reasons why people stuff their anger:

- They are afraid of hurting the other person or of being unable to handle the situation.
- They feel guilty or embarrassed about being angry.
- They are afraid of negative repercussions.

Stuffing sounds like a simple and effective way to avoid angry feelings, but it doesn't work. Stuffed anger breaks out in many different ways, and it can have very serious consequences. It spoils relationships, it harms your health, and it allows your anger and the riling circumstances to simmer on endlessly.

ESCALATING

Escalating is a style that attempts to shift the responsibility for an anger-provoking situation to someone else. Escalators accuse others, they swear, and they shout. Escalating doesn't work because it drives others away. It lets the objects of your anger off the hook because your behavior is so offensive and inappropriate that they become justified in not dealing with you. Note the paradox: The way the escalator tries to control the situation makes it worse. Escalators sometimes win their arguments, but their success is short-lived. Their targets may give in to avoid ugly confrontations, but in the long run they may try to get even. Like stuffing, escalating destroys relationships and is bad for your health.

Directing

Directing is a technique that uses anger in a carefully controlled manner to change the condition that is causing the anger. This technique is effective only when another person plays a role in provoking the anger. Directing has three simple steps:

1. You reveal the fact that you are feeling angry ("I feel angry . . .)
2. You identify the reason you are feeling angry (". . . that you did not run the project by me . . .)
3. You state the action that the other person could take to eliminate the provocation (". . . and in the future I would like you to check with me first before you go to senior management").

There are many benefits to directing your anger this way:

- You get your feelings off your chest without escalating.
- You get to the real cause of the problem.
- You decrease the chances that the same thing will happen again.
- Your honesty earns the respect of the other person.

Some people will be very uncomfortable when you direct your anger at them. These people will either avoid your attempts to deal with the issues or they will use techniques to deflect your approach. These techniques are called "blocking gambits" and they include:

- Making light of your anger by laughing it off or making a joke of it.
- Challenging the legitimacy of your anger.
- Putting you off until later.
- Threatening or personally attacking you.

- Questioning everything you say.
- Denying the validity of what you say.
- Trying to make you feel guilty.

When you encounter these blocking gambits, you cannot afford to let yourself become defensive too. Here are some ways to overcome others' blocking gambits:

- Repeat your statements calmly and clearly.
- Point out the fact that the person is avoiding the real issue by using blocking gambits.
- Appear cooperative by acknowledging the person's argument where it is valid while reiterating your own point of view.
- Ignore threats and get back to the point.

Your anger style usually depends on the circumstances and who is involved. Make a list of significant people you work with, and reflect on the anger style you use with each. You may stuff your anger with your boss but escalate with your subordinates. These observations will give you insights into the rules you use for anger expression and will help you make necessary changes to be more effective in anger expression.

Dealing with an Angry Person

I have given dozens of lectures and seminars on the popular management theme "Dealing with Difficult People." When I solicit a "Most Difficult People to Deal With" list, the first entry is usually people who are angry. Further exploration expands this question into: How do you deal with the person who responds with anger to your comments or actions . . . when they are angry at you? If they yell at you or maybe you know they are angry at you but they will not admit it? If they express anger at you in public, like at a staff meeting?

How do you help a person who is angry when you are not the source of their anger? If, for example, a co-worker is angry at a customer, what can you do to help?

It is clear to me why these are such popular questions. If someone you work with cannot handle her anger, it can create many problems—for you. If her anger is chronic, her performance suffers, which means that in some way or another, especially if you are in the same department or if the person is a boss or subordinate, your performance will inevitably suffer too. And your life, because of emotional contagion, will become a lot more difficult. Indeed, people rarely say that they like working with a person who can't manage his anger.

Let me tell you the methodologies I have found to be effective for three cases:

1. Coping with the person who directs his anger at you.
2. Helping the person whose anger is directed elsewhere.
3. Dealing with an angry group.

When You Are the Target of Anger

What can you do in the midst of a barrage of anger directed at you? How can you respond to make the exchange productive?

You have already taken the first step by learning how to manage your anger arousal and becoming more aware of your own feelings. This prevents escalation of the situation and increases your listening receptivity. Assuming that you are calm yourself, here are some specific ways you can respond that will help you deal with the person who is angry at you.

1. **Reduce his or her anger arousal.** This helps the angry person avoid intense anger arousal, making it easier to keep things "cognitively" in perspective. Do something that will relax the person. Actions that may be effective are:

- Getting the person to sit down or stop his or her present activity.
- Offering a drink of water or other noncaffeinated drink.
- Moving from the anger environment into another environment—conference room or office.
- Suggesting a ten-minute time-out.

All of these actions are based on the strategy of getting the individual to slow down his or her responses (thereby reducing anger arousal) without saying so. It is very important to remember that the individual's reactions are not something you can control. Therefore, it is quite possible that he or she will reject your efforts; the point, however, is that you still have options in how you respond. Your constant effort to relax the other will reflect your helping intent. You can also try the mood infection strategies suggested earlier.

2. **Hear the individual.** Listening to anger is much more than sitting down, being patient, and letting your boss blow off steam. Listening means making a concentrated effort to understand what your boss is angry about. Learning to listen is a skill that takes time and practice to develop, but here are some specifics that will help you get started:

- Do not interrupt. Interruption escalates a situation. It communicates that you are not listening. If you have the urge to interrupt, take a deep breath and remind yourself to listen.
- Do not mind read. There is a tendency to read into people's anger. If your boss is telling you he's angry because you missed a deadline, it does not mean he is going to fire you; he is simply expressing his anger. If you mind read, you will escalate the situation because you will respond to your mind-reading thoughts, which will be anger provoking.

- Be aware of your body language. Good eye contact and body posture are nonverbal signals that you are listening.
- Summarize in your own words what you think the individual is saying. Be sure to acknowledge his "right" to feel the way he does. Ask if you have captured the message. Now is the time, if you desire, to check out your mind-reading thoughts.
- If the person says you don't understand, explain that you want to. Ask for some examples to help clarify the issues. Make sure you take responsibility for not understanding. Saying "You don't make sense" will only escalate the situation or cause him to withdraw and intensify angry feelings.
- If the individual says you do understand, ask what can be done to resolve the situation. Agree to a solution only if you can implement it. Otherwise, the provocation will repeat itself, triggering more intense anger because you didn't follow through. When this happens, the person loses confidence in you and says things like "You always say you'll change, but you never do."
- If you disagree, it is still important to remember to validate his feelings. Responding with "You shouldn't feel that way" inevitably creates a power struggle that escalates the current "problem" and, in the long run, contributes to the anger affect. Better to help the person clarify expectations and counterpunch any cognitive distortions. Then focus on a solution that benefits the relationship, not just you.

HELPING OTHERS MANAGE ANGER

There are many times when your boss, co-worker, subordinate, or client is angry about things that have nothing to do with you. Nevertheless, their anger may still affect you, whether it is through emotional contagion or their impeded performance. For this reason alone, it is good business to help others manage their anger. Furthermore, you receive the additional benefit of increasing your skill in helping others deal with their emotions, feelings, and moods, an attribute that the successful individual possesses and one that is to become more and more important in the decades to come.

Here is how you can help others manage their anger when it is not directed at you:

1. **Recognize low levels of anger in others.** The better you become at recognizing low levels of anger, the easier it becomes for you to help others work them out. This is because you can intervene during the early stages of distress and help them before they get caught in the anger trap or begin to feel their situation is hopeless.

   Most people only recognize others' high levels of anger. One reason is that we don't recognize low levels of anger as being annoyance and irritation that can escalate into full-blown anger. Even low levels of anger cause unhappiness and disrupt performance.

   A good way to recognize a low level of anger is to pay attention to the words used. Angerologists agree that words used to describe anger correspond to the levels of anger experienced. For example, words that typically indicate a low level of anger are "bugged," "irritated," "bothered," "annoyed." Those representing a medium level are "angry," "mad," "upset," "pissed." And for a high level, you would hear "enraged," "furious," "livid."

   Of course, to accurately assess the other's anger level, you must take context into account. Tuning in to the words, however, will give you a good start to knowing when those around you are angry and approximately how angry.

2. **Communicate that you want to help.** Verbally communicate your desire to help. Respond in a way that invites your team member to share his feelings with you. These types of responses open the door for your co-worker by

signaling that you're willing to listen and help. Here are some examples of door openers:

Would you like to talk about it?
I would like to help you.
Tell me about it.
You can talk to me if you like.

3. **Help him problem solve.** Find out what happened; how he is thinking; what solutions, if any, he has tried. Your task is to help him generate effective responses and/or to reappraise the anger-provoking situation from a different perspective, one that is less anger provoking and one that he probably ignored in his initial anger reaction.
    Follow these conversational guidelines:

• Avoid verbal displays of impatience. This will demonstrate your willingness to help and give you the time you need to accurately hear the anger.
• Avoid blaming him for the "problem."
• Express open-mindedness, even toward irrational ideas.
• Make sympathetic remarks when appropriate.

These suggestions increase others' inclination to share their feelings with you because they see you are listening rather than blaming or evaluating them. Get them to realistically appraise their anger. When it's needless and unjust, simply talking about it will tend to dissolve it because you can help them clarify their cognitive distortions. When it's just, help them manage it by developing productive actions.

Most important, helping others manage their anger requires an attitude that implies willingness to give emotional support. People who give such support to their fellow workers usually find it is reciprocated.

A final point here is that sometimes others will not let you help them. If this happens, your best bet is to let them manage their anger on their own. Offer support when and if requested.

MANAGING AN ANGRY GROUP

Many people find themselves in the precarious position of having to face an angry group or, in some cases, a mob. Whether you're facing a union, protesters, a citizens' group, high school seniors, or a staff of twelve angry men, there are some steps you can take to prevent an explosion. Naturally, you begin by first managing yourself. Now try these actions:

1. **Quickly identify a common goal**, as this is one way you can unite yourself with the group. "We are all here because we recognize the importance of the issue and know we must productively resolve it."

2. **Clarify expectations** as to what the group can realistically expect to happen in the immediate future. Do not mislead them, as this will create expectations which, if not met, will only intensify the anger and cause you to lose credibility as a resolution force.

    You may also find it useful to explain what is not going to happen: "Well, we all know that this is not going to change by next week." A statement such as this is also a subtle way of getting the group to focus on the future rather than the here and now, which is where they are experiencing anger.

3. **Get the group involved** by listening. Give them plenty of time to vent their feelings, which you can summarize and reflect as a means to keep the anger at a manageable level. Remember the importance of validation. Avoid dialogues of a win-lose nature. Ask open-ended questions that will prevent you from polarizing yourself and the group.

4. **Help them problem solve** as you would help an individual. Identify what might work as well as what clearly won't or which actions might make the situation worse. The latter is a smart move because you are pointing out that destructive actions will not work, even if implemented. A high school principal, for example, when faced with five hundred angry high school seniors who thought smoking should be allowed in designated spaces said, "Burning a thousand packs of cigarettes in the schoolyard is not going to change anything." He added, "Besides, you'd be wasting your own smokes and money." Use "What if" questions, (e.g., What if we could smoke with our parents' permission?), as their answers will help you assess what will and will not reduce a group's anger.

5. **Provide opportunity** to follow up. Let the group know that resolution can take place only when there is a commitment by the parties involved. If the issues are unresolved, and most likely they will be, schedule a follow-up meeting, but this time, tell people to come with more workable plans and less anger. They need to know you want to help but need their help to do the job right.

Anger Management Communication Skills

Communication skills often come into play during an anger experience. Many times, it is either a poor use of the skill that triggers anger, or at other times using the skill effectively helps you manage the anger. Because these skills are powerful influences on the experience of anger, I refer to them as "anger communication skills" rather than as "conflict resolution skills," the conventional label. The subtle and important difference is highlighted by a few comments on the relationship between anger and conflict.

By definition, conflict exists when your goals/perceptions/feelings/etc. are incompatible with or in opposition to those of another. Many times you can be angry at another person and there is no interpersonal conflict. For example, you can be angry at a subordinate for a substandard presentation. He is angry too and acknowledges that he blew it. He also wanted a good presentation. There is no conflict between you but you are both experiencing anger.

Often, anger creates conflict. You are angry at your boss because you did not get a key assignment. Since you are a stuffer, you express your anger by avoiding him. You are now creating conflict fueled by your anger. Similarly, conflict can intensify your anger. Unable to resolve a disparity with a co-worker, you escalate the situation. Pretty soon, anger is soaring. Naturally, this increases the conflict.

Anger communication skills are those that help you manage the anger, not necessarily resolve the conflict. Remember, anger is an emotion and a conflict is a condition of interpersonal opposition. For sure, it is difficult to resolve conflict if the anger is not managed, and research tells us that if you do manage the anger, the chances for resolving a conflict are significantly increased.

The anger management communication skills are:

1. Assertiveness
2. Listening
3. Negotiation
4. Criticism
5. Confrontation
6. Praise

The goal here is to point out the role each skill plays in resolving the anger experience. This can be quickly accomplished.

ASSERTIVENESS

Assertiveness is the ability to express your feelings in a socially appropriate manner. Its chief function in managing anger is that it helps you stand up for yourself, to protect yourself, especially your self-esteem. This is particularly important when the provoking situation is one in which you are being abused or mistreated. Assertiveness in itself has been found to be effective in reducing anger and will be elaborated upon in the section on feelings.

Unfortunately, most people tend to confuse assertiveness with aggressiveness. While assertiveness is getting your needs met by expressing your feelings in an acceptable way, aggressiveness is the act of getting what you want at the expense of someone else. People who tend to be aggressive usually alienate those they deal with and create sources of anger around them.

Some questions to ask yourself that will help you implement assertive communication are:

- Am I expressing my feelings appropriately?
- Am I getting my needs met at the expense of others?
- Am I forcing my way on another?

LISTENING

We already know that when anger pollutes the air, it's tough to listen. But listen you must so that you can open up communication channels, something that is necessary if anger is to be resolved. Since listening plays a significant role in so many anger scenarios, we will look at the process in moderate detail.

Easier talked about than practiced, listening requires the ability to hear the content of the message and the feelings that often accompany it. Dynamic listening helps manage anger in a couple of ways: It allows you to understand and clarify the issues at hand, and it prevents anger from escalating because it makes you receptive to hearing the other's side rather than attacking him.

Most important, your listening to others serves as a validation of their feelings and thoughts. Indeed, validation of another's feelings has been found to reduce anger, even if the provoking situation or behavior doesn't change.

What makes it hard to listen? A major barrier is that every person has personal filters—attitudes, perceptions, feelings—that cause the listener in one way or another to shut down, inevitably making the other individual feel unheard and disgruntled. What are some of these filters that are activated in anger-provoking situations?

One is selectivity—the tendency to hear only what one wants to hear. The selectivity filter is often increased if the person is receiving unwanted news or information, which is usually the case when there is anger and conflict. The narrower the range of selectivity, the harder it becomes to hear the total message.

A second barrier is the "who" filter—the failure to hear the total message because one concentrates more on who is speaking than on what is being said. A manager, for example, will typically be more responsive to the same message if it comes from his boss rather than his subordinate.

Another potential hindrance to dynamic listening is the "Jack Webb" filter, which focuses strictly on the content—the desire for "nothing but the facts." This approach takes a very mechanistic view of the interaction. The energy of listening is expended toward the problem or the situation without much sensitivity to the sender of the message. This filter is used frequently by people who discount others' emotions or who are uncomfortable with their own feelings. An extreme example is the manager who, while drinking milk because of his ulcers, says, "We have to approach things around here rationally." The Jack Webb filter prevents him from seeing the value of intuitive insights or the positive benefits that can be derived from listening to and expressing emotions.

What can you do to decrease the likelihood that your personal filters will impede the communication process? How can you develop the skill of dynamic listening? Here is what I recommend:

- Be aware of your own filters. Question your own attitudes, beliefs, and perceptions before you try to resolve an interpersonal anger-provoking situation. Empty your head, as the Zen master would say.
- Silence. Simply saying nothing can be a way of assisting others. If one's silence is accompanied by appropriate nonverbal cues, i.e., direct eye contact, leaning forward, head nodding, the receiver will usually feel he is being listened to. This strategy also places the primary responsibility of disclosure on the sender of the message to share as little or as much as is comfortable.
- Restating information. Restating the information received from the sender provides the listener with the opportunity to check for accuracy in understanding the message. Most people feel listened to when the other person cares enough to respond intently. If used sincerely, the restating of information is an effective method of achieving dynamic listening.
- Reflecting feelings. In order to go beyond the surface of the sender's message, it is important to attempt to listen to the feelings behind what is being said. Reflecting, or sending back, the underlying feelings provides both the sender and the listener with the opportunity to engage in effective communication. Often, people simply need to "clear the air" by expressing their feelings and, in doing so, may resolve the original conflict.

NEGOTIATION

As a communication skill, negotiation is the process of two people modifying their positions for the purpose of coming to a mutually satisfying agreement. While each person is typically looking for her personal gain, the process is best served when each person gives up a little too.

Negotiation is a valuable anger management communication skill because it is the process that takes each person to the point that is needed to resolve the anger experience. It is most useful in situations where anger is provoked by interpersonal conflict and a change of behavior or position is required by both parties to resolve the conflict or anger experience. It may be between you and a co-worker about allocation of resources or between you and a client about a service provided. Whatever the conflict is, both parties will be required to negotiate if successful resolution is to be achieved.

Now the first problem. As any divorce attorney will tell you, when a person is angry, there is little chance that he is in a giving mood to the recipient of his anger. The attitude is solely "What can I get?" which usually increases the anger of the recipient. That in turn leads to a destructive power struggle, which leaves both parties cursing each other. Forget resolution, to say nothing of lost opportunities.

The second problem is to remember when you are angry, it is very difficult to appraise the situation from a different perspective, especially that of the individual sitting across from you. If you are locked into your perspective, it is quite reasonable to expect unreasonable demands and nonnegotiable items to quickly surface, items that if you were calm would be negotiable and facilitate resolution. Instead, your attitude angers and alienates the individual whom you need.

It is certainly good practice, therefore, not to negotiate when you are angry. But the truth is, this is usually not the case because the act of negotiating in itself often emerges when there is some type of conflict, whether it is international or in your office. You will inevitably have to negotiate while you are angry, albeit at a low or moderate level. So anger does not ruin your negotiation, practice these two points:

1. When you negotiate, focus on what you can give and still meet your objectives rather than focusing solely on what

you can get. Focusing on the other's needs will help keep your anger in check and prevent you from getting locked into focusing on your own needs.

2.   Always think about the other's perspective. Remember that two people can appraise the same event differently, but when you are angry you quickly forget this point. Thinking about the other's point of view will help you remember it, making you more apt to negotiate less pigheadedly and more effectively.

CRITICISM

Whether it is given or received, criticism often stirs anger in the workplace. Many times, criticism is motivated by anger, and then it is typically responded to in a defensive, if not overtly angry, manner. Yet productive criticism is a crucial skill for anger management because it becomes the means by which you can help somebody improve or change a vexing behavior. Changing and/ or improving an irritating behavior resolves the anger experience. The manager who knows how to productively criticize a subordinate for his anger-provoking behavior of being abrasive to him and his teammates not only manages anger in the workplace, but also nips his own anger in the bud.

The problem, of course, is that only a few know how to give or take criticism productively. Immediately begin to make criticism an anger management communication skill by doing two things:

1.   Change your perception of criticism. Think of it as a TASK—to Teach Appropriate Skills and Knowledge. This definition of criticism will keep your anger away because it will remind you that the goal of the criticism is to help develop, motivate, educate, and improve. You become less likely to use criticism as a way of expressing anger. Remember, it is always better to direct your anger

than to disguise it as "I'm telling you this for your own good," a common preface for criticism.

To solidify a productive criticism attitude, give yourself visual cues. Three- by five-inch cards or a sign behind your desk that says CRITICISM EQUALS TEACHING APPROPRIATE SKILLS will serve to remind you that criticism is not for expressing anger. One engineer told me he programmed his computer so the first message that came across his screen every day was "Criticism is information that can help me grow."

2. Always protect self-esteem. Criticism that threatens self-esteem—"This is terrible work"; "That was a stupid idea"—is sure to arouse anger. Criticism that protects self-esteem has a better chance of being acted upon and helps build a better relationship between you and the recipient. It makes it more probable that future anger-arousing incidents between the two of you will be handled fruitfully.

Some helpful tips to protect self-esteem when criticizing are:

- Use "I" statements instead of accusatory "you" statements.
- Avoid destructive labeling statements.
- Focus on how the person can improve rather than on what he did wrong.

CONFRONTATION

One of the most difficult and important anger management communication skills to master is that of confrontation, whose purpose is to acknowledge that a situation and/or behavior is not acceptable and cannot continue. The risk of a situation's getting worse or of a person's becoming defensive is usually present. Often individuals will claim that it is easier to let things go than to confront the person or situation directly. And they are right. In the short run, avoidance or stuffing is much easier. However, there will always be those instances in which, or individuals with whom, a showdown cannot be avoided.

The skills necessary for constructive confrontation include:

1. Taking responsibility for feeling that a situation or an individual's behavior is unacceptable.
2. Being specific in describing the unacceptable behavior or situation.
3. Stating clearly the tangible effects of the situation.

In contrast to this approach, most confrontations evolve into blaming sessions in which the chances for defensiveness and anger by all parties involved are greatly increased. I've been privy to many face-offs, and here is an example illustrating the differences between the two approaches:

Irresponsible confrontation: "You're late again and, as usual, inconsiderate about other people's feelings. You'll never know how to be responsible and will probably end up as the same lazy bum you are now!"

Responsible confrontation: "I'm really angry and disappointed that you're forty-five minutes late. This is the second time in a row you've been late and I've had to reschedule two appointments. I want you to know that this is completely unacceptable to me."

Needless to say, even with the most responsible of confrontations, the receiver is likely to become defensive and attack. If this occurs, the sender should try to listen effectively—which often defuses the anger—and repeat the responsible confrontation message. Note: Confrontation differs from directing anger in that its main intent is to stop a behavior from continuing. While that is also one purpose of directing anger, the intent of the latter is to simply communicate the feelings of anger, not necessarily change the anger-provoking situation.

PRAISE

Few people utilize praise in situations of anger and conflict. One reason is that when you are angry or in conflict with another, you focus on the negatives; you destructively label the person and/or situation. This makes it hard to commend another. A second factor is that after a conflict has been resolved, there are still some hurt feelings. Again, it is hard to praise another when you are having negative feelings.

Yet praise is a valuable anger management communication skill. It protects the other's self-esteem, giving him less reason to become defensive and remain angry. It is also a mechanism for maintaining positive changes that will prevent anger-provoking behavior from occurring in the future. Intermittently praising your subordinate for getting her work in on time is sure to rid her of the anger-provoking behavior of being late with her work. Praising a person shows you appreciate her and underlines the fact that you harbor no ill feelings. In essence, praise heals the wound of hurt and angry feelings.

Here are some guidelines for using praise effectively:

• Give praise only if you are sincere.
• Praise behaviors that make a difference.
• Be specific.
• Do it often.

Each of these six skills—assertiveness, listening, negotiation, criticism, confrontation, and praise—helps resolve anger and reduce interpersonal conflict.

You have probably noticed that these skills have common elements (for example, using "I" statements, taking responsibility for your feelings, being specific) yet each skill serves a different function in different circumstances. For example, while asserting yourself, directing your anger, and confronting another may sound the same, their intent differs. You assert to protect yourself—perhaps you will say you are angry. You direct to let another specifically know you are angry. You confront to tell another to stop a behavior. Understanding the function and intent of each skill is the key to making communication facilitate the anger management process.

Key Concepts: Communication is an important dimension and tool for managing anger. Unfortunately, anger and conflict distort the communication process. Sometimes the distortion is manifested by a restriction of information, as in stuffing. Other times, the distortion is demonstrated by intensifying the information, as in escalation. To prevent communication distortions from occurring, it is best to express anger directly. It is equally important to listen to the anger of others. This is especially crucial when dealing with an angry person or helping someone deal with anger and conflict that is not targeted at you.

Anger and
Feelings

Feelings. Whether it is understanding them, expressing them, or managing them, an ability to deal with one's feelings is a weak point for many of us. This is especially true for anger, a feeling that for most is usually too hot to handle.

In a work environment, dealing with feelings is easily mismanaged because most work environments hold to the assumption that displays or discussions of feelings are inappropriate.

This assumption puts us all in the position of not having a natural discourse for expressing our feelings—to do so would be hazardous to our job. Feelings are thought to be personal and private, to be dealt with at home, not in the work arena. Accordingly, displays and discussions of feelings are shunned, punished, or handled ineptly, unless of course it is a positive feeling expressed in an obvious situation, the proverbial slap-on-the-back, I'm-proud-of-you speech.

Feelings are part of being human and they inevitably will manifest themselves, maybe in disguised forms. When feelings are distressing, their disguise is usually villainous. For example, feeling bored or dejected at work, an employee might come in fifteen minutes late each day. Feeling jealous of a co-worker, a teammate might steal his rival's notes to sabotage him. Feeling angry at your boss, you might bad-mouth him. All of these feeling manifestations eventually lead to counterproductive results, to say nothing of impeded performance. This is the obvious consequence of mismanaged feelings.

There is another problem too. A larger one, perhaps a bit more existential. Most people report a sense of being disconnected at work. "Alone," "no trust," "empty," "lack of purpose," "tired," "burned out," "stuck" are some of the words I hear. Many people report they do not have "deep" relationships at work. "Businesslike," "superficial" are the adjectives individuals use to describe their relationships in the office. When someone perceives that his relationships are basically superficial, he is apt to feel not only alone, but also lonely. These feelings in turn stimulate other feelings of an even more distressful nature: anger, despair, and depression.

This should not be surprising since any personality theorist or mental health specialist will tell you that the desire to have relationships is a basic need of being human. Considering how much time you spend at work, it is only natural that the need to relate to others on more than a businesslike level surfaces. Yet when feelings are dismissed as being unimportant, they often are ignored and glossed over, making it impossible to have anything but superficial relationships. The point is not that feelings should always be expressed. This may or may not be true. The lesson here is more specific.

First, since feelings are part of the human experience and since they do impact your everyday functioning—as does anger—it is best to learn how to deal with all of your feelings more effectively, in ways that help you meet your psychological needs. People who are able to do this report that their relationships at work have greater meaning and are more pleasurable, which is less reported by those who express having difficulty in handling feelings at work.

Second, your lesson will illustrate how to use affective states to enhance your own effectiveness and the effectiveness of your organization. To do this, you need to learn something about the nature of feelings, gain some feeling awareness, and become adept in creating positive affect, a feeling state that enhances vital individual and organizational functions.

The Nature of Feelings

In their purest form, feelings represent the sensations we experience by touch. We assume that if we touch something, we know how it feels. In this context, physical touch helps us learn "feelings." For example, we can learn how cold feels by touching an ice cube or how lukewarm feels by dipping a hand in tepid water. We learn the "feel" of velvet by stroking it.

We touch thousands of things every day, yet it would be hard for you right now to get a good "feel" for each and every thing. For instance, what does your desk feel like? Can you get a good feel for its texture? Can you remember the feel of the fabric of yesterday's clothes? What does your spouse's hand feel like? These sensations often escape us, even when we are directly experiencing them. At the dinner table we are aware of the taste of "good" rather than being aware of how the table and chair feel. Sometimes, we're not even aware of our hand resting on somebody else's. Just because we're touching does not mean we're feeling.

Another way that we touch (and are touched by others) is through "psychological touches." A psychological touch occurs when an experience affects us, when it impresses us and changes our subjective experience of the world. Falling in love is being psychologically touched. So is being angry. Psychological touches differ from physical touches in that they do not necessarily involve making physical contact, although physical sensations are often the reference for psychological feelings. A shock from touching an electric wire or numbness of the mouth after a Novocain injection becomes a reference point for understanding the feelings of someone who says "I'm shocked" or "I'm numb." When we are psychologically touched, we experience a feeling.

Unlike physical touch, psychological touch is much more subjective because there is no direct physical or objective reference point, only your own perception. Psychological touch is also more lasting than physical touch. We all know that sometimes feelings last forever. This subjective viewpoint is the basis for the nature of your feelings. (In contrast, the basis for emotions are physiological arousal; emotions also tend to be shorter-lived than feelings.)

Nobody can tell you what you are feeling. Nor can anybody tell you why you feel a particular way, but people frequently try to do just that: "You feel so indifferent to me"; "You're angry at me because I was late."

Other times, people tell you that they don't know how you feel: "I never know what you're feeling. You never tell me how you feel." (Spouses often make this complaint about their partner; subordinates make it about their boss.)

These observations point up one of the major purposes for expressing feelings: They communicate to others the value that an experience has for us. How we are affected by what they do or say. How we are touched.

Despite the significance that feelings play in our lives, we do not always recognize them, let alone express them. More often than not, a subordinate will state that he feels okay about his performance appraisal, when in truth he is seething. The sales rep tells his boss he has shaken off his lost deal, when, in fact, he's depressed. Individuals have their own reasons for not recognizing or expressing their feelings, but there are general reasons.

For one thing, many of us are taught that feelings are unimportant, unpredictable, irrational, unfair, and potentially explosive, such as anger. If we exhibit angry feelings, we are seen as losing control, especially in the workplace. This becomes a conflictual situation because we are placed in the position of having feelings but are not encouraged to deal with them. It is very difficult to express and acknowledge our feelings when we are given so many messages to the contrary.

We also fail to acknowledge our feelings for fear of having to deal with the consequences they bring. This is very true in the work environment. I have heard many voice their experience that any expression of anger is usually met with negative repercussions ranging from losing resources to creating bad blood, a poor performance appraisal, and even to dismissal. Of course, many of these consequences stem from the way angry feelings are communicated, which is usually destructively.

Additionally, feelings of anger create the "anger affect"—other feelings that are uncomfortable: guilt, hurt, rejection, shame, embarrassment, hate, and even love. These feelings, which are the ones most of us experience after an emotional outburst of anger, are difficult to cope with because their subjective nature is distressful. Stuffing them becomes safer. You may tell your boss that everything is okay when you are really left with feelings of hurt and belittlement. Until you deal with the residue of these feelings created by the initial anger experience, anger will permeate the air. Similarly, many people do not acknowledge love because dealing with feelings of intimacy may be overwhelming. Feelings frighten us.

Sometimes we choose not to acknowledge or express our feelings because they make us vulnerable to hurt. In fact, the fear of being rejected is perhaps the major reason why we hesitate to express our feelings. These concerns are real and make a valid point: After we are aware of our feelings, it is our choice whether and how we express them. Indeed, it would be unwise not to acknowledge that revealing feelings at work can be risky.

Feeling Awareness

Before you can learn to use your feelings productively, you have to acknowledge them. Some feelings are easier to acknowledge than others. It is a lot easier, for example, to acknowledge that we are feeling happy than that we are feeling sad. Positive feelings are pleasant; negative ones may hurt us.

I have noted that many people confuse feelings with thinking or observation:

"I feel it wasn't right that you didn't call me."

"I feel that you are lying to me."

"I feel you don't love me."

"I feel it wasn't right." How can that be? How can we feel "It wasn't right"? Right is not a feeling. It is an evaluative thought. We frequently express our feelings the way we would thoughts because we don't know exactly how to describe them when we experience them. Feelings expressed like thoughts are known as I-feel-thinking statements rather than as I-feel-emotion statements. A good rule for whether you are making an I-feel-thinking statement is to replace "I feel" with "I think." If it makes sense, then it is probably a thinking statement rather than a feeling-emotion statement (i.e., "I think it wasn't right that you didn't call me" makes sense). The previous I-feel-thinking statements can be changed to I-feel-emotion statements:

"I feel hurt that you didn't call me."

"I feel frustrated that you are lying to me."

"I feel sad that you don't love me."

Recognizing I-feel-thinking statements is important because it's a cue that indicates you are having difficulty in expressing feelings. When you are able to change I-feel-thinking statements to I-feel-emotion statements, you communicate more accurately to your self and others what you are experiencing. Knowing what you are experiencing allows you to get a handle on your feelings.

Given all these obstacles and problems, why should you want to be more aware of your feelings? You've already heard part of the answer. Feelings provide you with important information about yourself and your judgment of whatever situation you are in. Also, there is enough research to confidently say that people who make decisions using both thinking and feeling responses are more likely to be happier with their results.

Being aware of your feelings will also prevent you from feeling worse. If you have lost a big account or made a poor presentation, it is hard to deal with the feelings of anger, hurt, and rejection you may feel. If you choose to deny these feelings, you will feel worse. Expressing these feelings allows you to move on with your business. For example, engineers who have been laid off and given an opportunity to express their angry feelings found the layoff to be less stressful than engineers who were not provided the same opportunity.

Another important reason to be aware of your feelings and to be able to express them is that it fosters psychological intimacy. While you can certainly survive in a world of superficial businesslike relationships, it would be difficult for you to thrive. When you acknowledge how you feel, you are sharing your very own perceptions of the world with someone else. In a sense, you are inviting a person into your world. There is absolutely no doubt that people who share feelings have a better chance of having a productive relationship. Subordinates and bosses who share their feelings of anger, anxiety, and enthusiasm with each other report having better relationships than their counterparts who do not disclose their feelings; the same is true for peers.

In addition, being aware of feelings and expressing them allows you to be real, to be yourself. By being yourself, you don't communicate confusing messages that inhibit trust.

What can you do to become more aware of your feelings and express them so they reflect what you experience? You've already taken the first step if you've been expanding your self-awareness by monitoring yourself and gathering mood information. Keep a Feeling Journal. At the end of the day or at different times of the day, make a note of what feelings you have experienced in the preceding hours. Doing this on a daily basis will increase your awareness of how and what you feel each day. If you scoff at this task, consider that first-year MBA students at Northwestern University (a preeminent business school) are required to keep a Feeling Journal for their first year. Purpose: to become more aware of their feelings and the role they play in their work.

Another assignment that helps improve feeling awareness is to build I-feel-emotion statements into your daily conversation. Talking about feelings makes you more aware of what you are feeling.

You may also increase your awareness of feelings by paying attention to the physical feels you have every day. Give yourself assignments of touching something smooth, soft, hard, etc. Studies show that as physical sensitivity increases, so does psychological sensitivity. It is also a good exercise to ask others how they feel. This not only gives you practice in listening to others, but also creates the expectation that it is okay to talk about feelings, especially at work.

Expressing Feelings

After becoming aware of your feelings, the next step is learning how to express them.

Contrary to conventional wisdom, we almost always express our feelings. Sometimes we do it directly, while at other times, usually in work environments, we do it indirectly—by tone of voice, body posture, eye contact, or facial expression. A co-worker who always comes to meetings late or constantly puts down your ideas is expressing her feelings—just not directly. Many times, particularly with anger, we hide our feelings by saying something that is very different from what we feel. The majority of time, for example, subordinates will tell their boss that they are not angry over a change in plans, that they understand, rather than state that they are angry. Actions like this lead to confusion since what we say is contradicted by our behavior, voice, or gestures. Hidden feelings may protect us, but when there is confusion in a relationship, there is little chance for trust. Having a productive relationship and being who we are depends on communicating our feelings clearly.

To give yourself feeling expression training, remember to use your I-feel-emotion statements daily. It is also useful to make a list of different feelings you experience and then to think about how you show them in different daily encounters with your boss, peers, and customers. Review the section on assertiveness.

There is one more important point to make about your feelings. Although you have the right to express your feelings, you do not have the right to expect other people to change because of the way you feel. They may choose not to change, even after you have said that you feel bad about something they are doing. You can't force someone to change. If your boss or top client decides to change his behavior, it is because he sees who you are and because he cares about how you feel. In short, you need to trust his goodwill toward you. If your trust is low, begin to build it up by acknowledging your feelings and expressing them directly. Remember, where feelings aren't voiced clearly, a quality relationship is impossible.

Making Feelings Work for You

You can use affective states—positive and negative feelings—productively. So you can see the rationale of my recommendations, I will first familiarize you with the study of positive affect.

POSITIVE AFFECT: COOKIES AND KINDNESS

In recent years, social psychologists have directed increasing attention to the impact of affective states on behavior and cognition. While such research has examined the effects of both positive and negative affect, findings regarding the former have generally been much more consistent. For this reason, I will focus primarily on the influence of positive affect and how you can use it for improving individual and organizational effectiveness.

Many intriguing results have been obtained in experiments addressing the topic of positive affect. It has been found, with respect to interpersonal behavior, that people are generally more helpful and cooperative and less aggressive when they are in a positive mood than when they are in a neutral one. Results related to cognition indicate that even relatively mild shifts in affect can influence several important processes, including memory and creativity. Subjects are, for example, more apt to be original in their thinking when they are in a positive mood.

Given the generality of the findings, it seems only reasonable to assume that they might be relevant to several processes occurring in work settings. This is exactly the case. The way individuals feel does influence several important forms of work-related behavior. Specifically, positive affect has been found to influence processes fundamental to organizational functioning, from decision making and innovation to group cohesiveness and interpersonal relationships. Let me give you a few examples and implications.

Positive Affect and Negotiations

Would you rather negotiate with someone who is irritable or with someone who is feeling good? The answer is obvious: An opponent who is experiencing positive affect would be a better bet for reaching an amicable agreement.

Studies show this to be true. For example, in one of the experiments dealing with affective states, subjects played the roles of buyer and seller and bargained over the price of several items (television sets, typewriters, vacuum cleaners). Before the start of negotiations, some subjects were exposed to events designed to put them in a good mood (they rated some funny cartoons or received a small gift). Others were not exposed to such treatment.

The experimenters predicted that those who had been placed in a positive mood would be more likely to reach an optimal agreement (one that maximized the joint outcomes of both persons) and to have more favorable evaluations of both the situation and their opponent. In addition, subjects in a positive mood were expected to be less likely to engage in contentious tactics—efforts to defeat or intimidate their opponent. Results confirmed these predictions.

Considering the frequency and importance of negotiations in most organizations, these findings have several practical implications. One is that it is probably good business to take steps to put one's opponents in a good mood. Indeed, any costs involved may well be more than offset by the gains made by relatively smooth and speedy progress toward a workable agreement. A second implication is to be on guard when your opponent attempts to put you in a good mood.

Positive Affect and Job Interviews

You're on a job interview. You enter the room, and you can immediately tell the interviewer is in a bad mood. How would you react to this? Probably with dismay because you would realize the interviewers's negative feelings might lead her to evaluate you more harshly than would otherwise be the case. Conversely, if you found that this person was in a positive mood, you would presumably be happy because you would realize the interviewer's positive feelings might lead her to judge you more favorably.

The findings of several recent studies indicate your thoughts are accurate. For example, in one investigation of this topic, the experimenters asked interviewers in a leadership training program to rate their own affective states after conducting interviews with prospective candidates. Results showed that the more positive the interviewer's reported mood (positive affect), the greater his tendency toward leniency in his ratings; that is, the greater the propensity to assign higher ratings to the applicants than they really deserved. In related studies, researchers also found that when individuals are induced to experience a special type of positive affect—liking for another person—they tend to rate him or her more favorably—but perhaps less accurately—than when such affect is not present.

Clearly, it is important for interviewers and anyone else who assesses others' qualifications or performance to be aware of such effects. If they are not, the result may be errors in hiring, promotion, and related decisions—errors that can prove costly to both the organizations and the individuals involved.

Positive Affect and Risk Taking

Are you more willing to take a risk when you are in a good mood or a neutral one? If you are in a good mood, do you want to keep it by avoiding possible loss? After all, taking a risk does involve potential loss.

Systematic research indicates that both patterns are valid, but only under somewhat different conditions. Specifically, persons experiencing positive affect are more willing to take risks when the potential losses involved are small or trivial. They are less willing to take risks when potential losses are significant and they think about these. Both patterns have recently been demonstrated and under the expected conditions.

Researchers first placed subjects in a good mood by providing them with a small, inexpensive gift and then measured their willingness to take risks under two sets of conditions. In one situation, potential losses were small, and subjects were induced to concentrate on possible gains by indicating how much they would pay for lottery tickets that might enable them to win cash prizes. Here, people in a good mood were willing to pay more than those in a neutral mood. Moreover, the greater daring of subjects in a good mood increased as the chances of winning and the size of the prizes available rose. In another situation, potential losses were large, and subjects were induced to concentrate on these by indicating how much they would pay for insurance to protect themselves against the loss of valuable items. Here, persons in a good mood were willing to pay more for the insurance. Again, the tendency to avoid risk increased as the size of the potential losses increased.

Together these findings support the reasoning outlined above: People in a good mood are more inclined to take risks, provided that potential losses are unlikely or small in magnitude. However, they actually become less willing to take risks than those in a neutral mood when potential losses are probable or large, and they dwell on these negative outcomes.

This pattern has important applications for people in work settings who must make decisions involving risk. Individuals whose jobs include this type of responsibility should avoid making risk-related decisions at times when they are elated. Under such conditions, they may tend to choose courses of action that have relatively high levels of risk, or at least levels they would find unacceptable at other times.

One method to counter such effects would be to build in safeguards designed to emphasize potential losses. As noted above, attention to losses tends to counter or even reverse inclinations toward risk on the part of persons experiencing positive affect. In any case, it appears that positive affect is one more factor that can serve to distort the judgment of decision makers. Its impact should not be overlooked in situations in which the stakes, for individuals, groups, or organizations, are high.

Positive Affect and Job Satisfaction

When we are in a good mood, we have a tendency to view the world through rose-colored glasses, to evaluate many events and experiences more favorably than we would otherwise.

Systematic research confirms this impulse, suggesting that people in a good mood do indeed assess relatively neutral or ambiguous stimuli more favorably than persons not in a good mood. Again, we may ask, are such effects related to important aspects of work behavior? You know the answer is yes.

People in a good mood tend to rate their jobs (and specific aspects of them) more positively than those not in a good mood. For example, one experimenter had male and female subjects perform a task in which they coded information about twenty imaginary candidates for teaching associate positions at a large university. Subjects performed this task in two different ways: They were either given the applications and told how to code the information (the unenriched version) or they were allowed to select the applications they wished to code and permitted to enter the information in any way they wished (the enriched version). In addition, before beginning work, half of the subjects were exposed to conditions designed to generate positive affect (they saw amusing comedy films); the remaining subjects did not have this experience. After working on the tasks, subjects rated them on several dimensions (e.g., their seeming importance, the extent to which they provided them with variety, and autonomy).

The experimenters predicted that subjects would report more favorable reactions to the enriched version of the task than to the unenriched version (this would merely confirm the findings of previous research on job satisfaction). In addition, the researchers predicted that subjects experiencing positive affect would also evaluate the tasks more favorably than those in a more neutral mood. Both predictions were confirmed. It also appeared that at least for some measures of a subject's reactions, the influence of positive affect was stronger for the enriched than for the unenriched version.

Other evidence suggests that positive and negative affect may even play a role in absence from work. The more positive the feelings individuals report having while at work, the lower their rate of absenteeism. Apparently, when being on the job is associated with positive feelings, people act on this relationship by regularly showing up for work. When, in contrast, they experience mainly negative feelings, they stay away—and so avoid at least one source of irritation. Of course, many factors besides temporary moods influence individuals' decisions to attend or be absent from work. Economic necessity, health, family obligations, and a host of other variables enter the picture. Still, it appears that affective reactions to one's job and work environment can have important effects and should be taken into account in efforts to enhance productivity.

INDUCING POSITIVE AFFECT IN WORK SETTINGS

Admittedly, this discussion of positive affect has touched on many topics and reviewed a wide range of research findings. I know it will be very useful to show how the beneficial effects described earlier may actually be realized in many work settings. This issue in turn leads to an essential question: How can positive affect be induced among individuals at work? Several techniques, many of them suggested by the findings of social pyschology, appear to be potentially useful. I'll go from the general to the specific.

First, efforts to induce positive affect among working people might focus on improving the physical environment. A large body of research in social psychology suggests that people's feelings, moods, social behavior, and task performance are all affected by a number of environmental variables: temperature, lighting, air quality, noise. Moreover, related findings indicate that such factors also influence reported job satisfaction and motivation.

Improvements in these conditions can be costly; soundproofing, air-conditioning, improved heating all represent substantial capital costs. Yet given the many benefits that may follow from the positive shifts in affect they produce, such investments may well prove worthwhile. In addition, some evidence indicates that mild increments in positive affect can be obtained through relatively inexpensive means. One recent study suggests that most individuals experience positive affect when they are in the presence of pleasant artificial scents. In addition, this fragrance-generated positive affect is then reflected in increased self-confidence, higher self-set goals, and greater willingness to cooperate with others. Of course, such findings are only preliminary; further research is needed before the potential usefulness of such interventions can be determined.

A second and different approach to inducing positive affect in the work setting is suggested by a basic finding of social and clinical psychology: In most cases, people strongly prefer to have a degree of control over important events in their lives. When this is not the case, feelings of anger, depression, and helplessness quickly emerge.

This principle suggests that employees will experience higher levels of positive affect (and lower levels of negative affect) when they are permitted to take part in decisions affecting their jobs. Such participative decision making has been found to enhance both job satisfaction and output. It seems possible that such effects stem at least in part from the positive affect individuals experience when they know that their opinions and preferences are being heeded in an otherwise autocratic system. It is interesting to note that while most companies state that the employees actively participate in their performance appraisal, the majority of employees believe that their input has little effect on the outcome of that performance rating.

Many organizations have a corporate culture—shared beliefs, values, and expectations—that contains attitudes about employees that may expose them to unnecessary levels of stress, interfere with effective communication, and generally convey the message that subordinates are not to be trusted or are not competent and that managers are present to check up on them and goad them into doing their jobs. Not all organizations have such cultures, of course, but many do possess at least some of these negative features.

Therefore, organizations can raise positive affect and minimize negative affect by eliminating unnecessary causes of stress (for example, inequity of treatment, poor physical surroundings, withholding vital information) and by focusing on the organizational culture. A culture that fosters a positive attitude toward employees and expectations about their motives and competencies may actually lead to enhanced positive affect in the workforce. Needless to say, such a goal is easier to state than to attain.

What can you do as an individual to make positive affect work for you? Try these recommendations:

1. Keep yourself in a positive mood. Use your self-statements to help you wear your COTE of armor—Confidence, Optimism, Tenacity, and Enthusiasm. Such a suit makes you and those around you feel good. Remember that emotional contagion may be at work.

2. Induce positive affect in others. You can make others feel good by giving praise and compliments (remember to be specific). These acts of recognition elevate an individual's self-esteem and create positive feelings. The same is true when you listen to others. Your dynamic listening communicates that you are genuinely focused on them and validates their feelings, something that makes us all feel

better. Also, use emotional contagion principles to infect enthusiasm.

3. Find everyday uppers. Be alert to little things that you can build in to your daily work life that make people feel good. I've noticed a few that seem to generate good feelings at work. One is food. Whether it is a coffee cake every morning for the staff or a box of cookies given out once a month, eating and receiving food seems to make people feel good. (Unfortunately, I don't think carrots and celery would do the job.)

4. Offer help whenever you can. This tends to build goodwill and cooperative relationships that you will need later. Offering help also communicates your positive attitude toward fellow workers.

5. Be kind. Several studies show that managers who are kind to their subordinates end up with a more productive staff.

For the real "how-toers" I offer these positive affect interventions:

*   The next time you are being evaluated or interviewed, try to get the individual in a good mood. If you are subtle and effective, you may get a point or two.
*   When you are negotiating, don't be elated. You may lose. You need to reduce your positive feelings so that you can be more objective in your task. Better to think of potential loss and a few negatives about your adversary—all for the purpose of getting the best deal for you and your organization.
*   When you are giving a performance appraisal, put the recipients in a good mood. Get them involved by listening to their concerns and developing goals and action plans. Their positive feelings will make it easier for them to listen to your views, making differences easier to resolve.
*   Want your staff to have greater job satisfaction and enjoy-

ment? Create meaning in their jobs. Tell them why it is important and how it affects operations.

- Want your client to buy? Get him to reminisce with one of his favorite stories. He might just end up ordering more than you expected.
- Want your sales reps to do well? Send them off to work with a good joke and a verbal vote of confidence.

As you start to make positive affect principles work for you, I think you will make two observations. First, I believe you will see yourself and your organization become more effective. Second, I believe you will feel better and be happier at work. In essence, your feelings will be working for you.

Key Concepts: Contrary to conventional wisdom, feelings are an important factor in the world of work for two reasons. First, they provide a major avenue for relating to others. Everybody has feelings, and it is a natural desire and need to have relationships in which feelings are conveyed accurately. This is especially true in our work environments and relationships when we consider how much time we spend at work or with our job colleagues. When feelings are ignored or minimized, it is only natural for individuals to feel alone, disconnected, misunderstood, or angry.

The methodology for handling feelings at work includes gaining awareness of your feelings, deciding whether or not it is beneficial to express those feelings, and introducing "feeling talk" into your conversation. One thing is for sure: It is very difficult to have a productive relationship with anybody if feelings—both positive and negative—aren't communicated.

The second reason feelings are important in the work environment is the fact that affective states do influence many key aspects of job performance. By inducing positive feelings in individuals, you can influence their job performance.

Since everybody has feelings and since feelings do affect job performance, it is the wise individual who begins to make feelings work for him or her.

Anger and
Behavior

Behavior is what you do. It is your actions, the responses you gener-ate. On the job, it is your behavior that is watched. It is your behavior that counts. It is your behavior that is appraised. Nobody gets in trouble for thinking about punching his boss. Act on the thought and it's a different story.

Think of the last time you were angry. How did anger affect your behavior? What did you do? Were your actions productive? Did they help you manage the provocation? Most people, be they at home or at work, act counterproductively when angry. The behaviors range from drinking, smoking, and compulsive eating to murder in the post office. In between, there are millions of others whose "anger actions" impede their own success.

The baseball pitcher argues with the first-base umpire and becomes tuned out to the fact that two runners are crossing home plate. The sales rep is angry at a client, so he delays in calling him back for just the length of time the client uses to find another supplier. The subordinate hands in a piece of work late to make his boss look bad, even though he knows he will suffer worse consequences. An employee whose effectiveness depends on communicating with her peers avoids speaking to her teammate because she is angry about his tardiness. Do you think that these are actions to take to manage anger productively? These are, however, frequent examples of how people actually act when they are angry on the job.

While it is very difficult to change your behavior, especially anger actions, it can be done. You can learn how to transform your anger actions into productive behavior, the bottom line in being a successful anger manager. What is required is knowing a little about psychological learning principles—how to stop anger actions from occurring and how to generate productive behaviors that will resolve anger-provoking encounters. (Studies show that modifying behavior often leads to a change in thinking. Just as you can manage your behavior through cognitive interventions, so you may also manage your thinking through productive actions. This is another example of how the dimensions of anger—cognitive and behavioral—interact with each other.) To change your anger actions, proceed at once.

Learning Our Anger Actions

A good place to start is to get a behavioral overview of how we learn our anger actions—the behaviors we do when we are angry. As you know, how you respond is influenced by many factors, including cognitive appraisal. I want to illuminate the importance of two psychological learning principles, for it is these processes that are generally regarded as the major factors in shaping our actions when we are angry.

MODELING

Psychological research has taught us that observing other people can teach us what to do and how to do it. The girl who learns how to calm her baby brother by watching her mother is using modeling. The father who teaches his daughter to serve a tennis ball by saying "Watch me first" is using modeling. Unfortunately, in the case of anger we frequently model behavior that has counterproductive results for ourselves and others.

How did your parents, brothers, and sisters act when they were angry? Chances are that if your parents expressed anger through yelling, name calling, or sarcasm, you probably do the same. If your parents responded to anger by leaving the room, your reactions are likely to be similar. You have learned these patterns by observing others. By observing the actions of others we see how our society manages anger. Naturally, we deduce that anger is a negative event.

Likewise, when a senior manager gets angry and yells at his associate for missing a deadline, he not only makes the situation worse (behavior effecting anger), but he also gives the associate the message it is okay to yell at someone when you are angry. It should not be surprising if that very same employee goes on to yell at his own subordinate, probably for missing a deadline. You can count on the fact that during the associate's performance appraisal, he will be told that he must control his anger and learn how to communicate more effectively with his subordinate.

Applying modeling to managing anger on the job should be obvious: Show them the way, walk the talk. Model the actions you want others to take when they are angry. Two requirements: You must be aware of what behaviors you need to model, and you must have the opportunities to expose others to them.

Begin by becoming aware of what you do when you are angry. If you find these actions counterproductive, you'll have to change them, perhaps by using one of the behavioral interventions soon to be discussed. The objective is to stop doing what you don't want others to do when they are angry.

Next, ask yourself, "How do I want my staff to act when they are angry?" This will require some thought. You may even con-sider asking others for their thoughts on the subject. I have seen many successful anger managers turn this question into a produc-tive staff discussion. Once these actions are enumerated, you must act them out and point them out to others.

For example, let's say you are at a staff meeting and, in typical manner, a colleague has insulted you. Your usual response has been to stuff your anger. Besides the negative consequences of that, your stuffing also communicates to your colleagues that the "model" way for the team to handle anger is to stuff it. On the other hand, if you respond by blending assertiveness and con-frontation—"John, I am angered by your insults and really do not appreciate them. If you would like to discuss it further, I'm avail-able"—you not only increase the likelihood that you will dimin-ish your colleague's insults, but also communicate a very different message to the rest of the team.

Through your actions, you are saying it is okay to be angry, it is okay to express it, and your effective response models how to do it. (This example shows again how different dimen-sions of anger interact with each other: Here, the behavioral dimension is the act of communicating; the content is a re-flection of the communication dimension. Together they in-teract for a productive action. In contrast, if the act of communicating stayed constant but the communication di-mension reflected an escalating style, anger actions would be sure to result.)

Here is another example. You are in your office with a sub-ordinate, and you get an unexpected cancellation from an im-portant client, the third time in a row. Instead of the proverbial curse-out, you'd be much better off taking advan-tage of the situation. "I'm really angry at this guy. I think I'll have to speak to him about billing for cancellations or impose some other penalty. What do you think?" You have appropri-ately modeled expressing angry feelings as well as shown your employee that part of managing anger is formulating a productive action plan. And, most important, you have turned the anger experience into a teaching opportunity by asking your subordinate how she would respond, how she would manage her anger. This example again highlights the importance of being aware of those times when you are angry. If not, you could not take advantage of such an event.

Depending on many factors, including your position and status at work and the relationship you have with your fellow workers, there is a chance that others model your productive anger actions. Even if this is not the case, you are still acting productively when you are angry.

OPERANT LEARNING

A second psychological learning principle that helps explain the shaping of our "angry behavior" is operant learning. Our behavior "operates" on our environment (or another person) to produce specific results—we take an action and see what occurs. If our behavior produces desirable results, we tend to repeat it. If the results of our actions are undesirable, we don't repeat the behavior.

Examples of operant learning are all around us. The child learns to use a Frisbee by throwing it in different ways until he discovers the way to pitch it with accuracy; he then knows how and can do it again. Mixing a recipe to taste is operant learning, too. Sometimes we get the results we want on the first try. Other times, we try a hundred variations before we get what we want. In any case, the action that we "keep" is the one that succeeds.

Many of us have learned our patterns for how to act when we are angry through operant learning. A man may discover that if he doesn't want to hear his wife's concerns, all he has to do is insult her and she will back off. The fact that his wife always reacts in the same way serves to increase the probability that he will insult her in the future whenever she voices her criticism. Although his insults are hardly productive for their marriage in the long term, he does get a desirable immediate result: His wife stops nagging him. His wife meanwhile "learns" that if she walks out of the room, she won't have to hear his insults. Her behavior, too, produces a desirable effect. Because they both get what they want, at least temporarily, their actions will tend to be repeated.

In the same way, a worker may learn that if he responds to his co-worker's criticism with anger and retaliatory aspersions, the issue is dropped. An engineer working in a manufacturing plant makes the point by writing on an anger questionnaire: "For years, I responded to my colleagues' criticism with anger. I found it to be a pretty effective way to keep them silent and their noses out of my work. It wasn't until years later that I realized I was hurting myself. I probably lost plenty of opportunities to improve my work by responding so counterproductively." During those years, his co-workers learned that withholding their criticism was the best response since it ensured that they would not have to deal with his wrath.

This example illustrates an important paradox about operant learning in the context of anger. Because unproductive responses are somewhat reinforced—many times the yelling or sulking gets you what you want—it is difficult to conceive of trying new ways of responding, even though these new ways would yield better results. Consequently, the negative pattern continues, becoming stronger and stronger and more habitual. The pattern inevitably feeds on itself. Every time your subordinate is late with a project, you automatically scream. Every time your boss criticizes your performance, you automatically avoid him for a week and lash out at your assistant. Since each of these anger actions provides some quick relief, it will most likely be your first response when-ever the provocation is encountered. In essence, your behavior is keeping you stuck; your anger actions are self-perpetuated.

There is also another way that operant learning shapes anger actions. Many times, we reinforce behavior in those we live and work with that we later find provoking us to anger. The boss who tells his subordinate not to worry that his report was a few hours or even a day late is in effect reinforcing that it's okay to be late. Six months later at a performance appraisal, the first problem brought up is the subordinate's tendency to be late on his projects.

What might you do to make operant learning work for you? You have to reinforce those behaviors you want more of and discourage those you want to occur less frequently, if at all.

Unfortunately, this is not so easy to do because it presupposes that you know what you want to do when you are angry and what you want others to do when they are angry. Do you? If not, ask others what they think and act on the earlier suggestion of turning it into a staff discussion. Be sure to share your own views, as this will give you an opportunity to acknowledge that you too get angry and make it easier for others to share their thoughts and feelings. Some questions to ask:

- How do all of you handle anger? What do you do?
- What do you see others do when they get angry?
- How do you respond to others' anger?
- How do you want others to respond to yours?
- What do you like others to do when they are angry?
- How do you encourage people to handle anger productively?

A bank manager using this procedure collected the following suggestions:

- "Have a co-worker productively express her anger at your neglecting to pass on an important message. Thank her for being professional for telling you and give reassurance that you won't make the mistake again."
- "When your team members work out their differences, remember to praise their excellent ability to do so and remind them how important this is to their effective functioning." Reward them with cookies.
- "Help another person act productively by being sensitive to his anger."

- "If you think somebody is angry at you, approach her. Don't wait for her to approach you."

Also note that interventions such as these not only help you determine cultural guidelines for behavior when angry and how to deal with inappropriate anger expression, but also get people to talk about anger; that is, their feelings and emotions.

You can also use operant learning to manage anger by changing how you respond to anger-provoking behavior in others. Again, you need to identify those aggravating behaviors, examine how you traditionally respond to them, and then generate a different response that changes the behavior, or as a behaviorist would say, extinguishes it. Two short examples: Tell your subordinate that it is important to get his work in on time (otherwise, his perform-ance is impeded) rather than, "Don't worry about it." Assert, confront, and criticize your boss about his abrasive behavior in-stead of ignoring it, which reinforces him to stay the same. Use your discretion and best judgment as to when to do this—in private or in a staff meeting, or at all.

Modeling and operant learning are not quick fixes. Changing behavior takes time, and during this time you must be consistent or else old, counterproductive patterns will reemerge. What hap-pens when this occurs? Anger immediately will become destruc-tive and will probably sabotage your effort to become an anger manager.

DE-ESCALATING ANGER: TIME OUT

You cannot stop everyone's anger from getting out of control. Conflict, especially in any team environment, is inevitable, and how individuals deal with their own anger and conflicts is to a wide degree out of your control.

But you can stop the anger from being destructive in those situations that involve you. Remember, anger tends to feed on itself and to escalate. This is especially true when two or more people are involved in a confrontation that makes one or both of them feel threatened. Once the escalation process begins, it is difficult—if not impossible—to think and act rationally unless something is done to defuse the situation.

You can do this by calling a "time-out." This behavioral intervention removes you completely from the provocative situation and gives you an opportunity to manage the reactions—especially the anger arousal—that you are experiencing. The time-out procedure is very simple:

- You let the other person or persons know that your anger is building ("I am beginning to feel very angry . . .").
- You declare your desire to remove yourself from the situation temporarily (". . . and I want to take a time-out").
- You remove yourself immediately.

Your time-out should last for exactly one hour. Leaving the length open-ended makes it too easy to avoid the problem indefinitely, and also puts the other parties at an unfair disadvantage by leaving them in midair and at your mercy.

During the time-out, you should do something constructive rather than focusing on your anger. Doing something physical—for example, busywork like cleaning out your files, getting your desk in shape—will help you get rid of some of your angry tension as well as helping you regain your composure, to say nothing of actually getting some work done. Using relaxation techniques will help you restore calm to your mind.

After one hour, you should attempt to resume the discussion. A good place to start is by talking about why you called the time-out and how you felt during it. If the other party doesn't want to resume the discussion immediately after the time-out, try to set a mutually agreeable time for talking.

Some anger-provoking situations may be too sensitive to return to in an hour. When that's the case, set another time in the not-too-distant future to deal with the matter. Whatever you do, don't drop the subject and pretend that the anger will go away.

Using that approach will just set you up to suffer in the future from past resentment and bitterness, feelings that keep anger alive.

THE CREATIVE TIME-OUT

What about those times when you get angry at a staff meeting or in a performance appraisal? It is probably unrealistic to think that you can simply walk away for an hour or even twenty minutes. In instances such as these you need to be creative and think of something that you can do to prevent things from escalating. For example, while you cannot leave the situation for an extended time, you can excuse yourself for a quick trip to the bathroom. Dab some water on your neck or wrists (remember, you are hot under the collar) to cool off, and return to the scene. Or you might say, "Look, this is really important. I just want to tell my assistant to hold my calls." The minute or two it takes to do this helps interrupt the anger experience.

How could you use the creative time-out if you witness two of your subordinates getting ready to escalate in a staff meeting? You could say, "Hey, don't get angry," but it has been my experience that this may add fuel to the fire because it may elicit defensiveness from your subordinates or, at the very least, embarrass them for losing their cool. Instead, use the technique of reframing: "Hey, I appreciate the enthusiasm that is being shown. Let's take a break and then we will pick it up again." Here, you have "reframed" anger as enthusiasm, thus allowing everybody to save face and regain his composure. What makes this effective in this example is that the physiological arousal associated with enthusiasm is similar to anger arousal. Therefore, the alternative explanation created by the reframing becomes believable: "Gee, I am enthusiastic about this particular point."

Whatever the situation, just remember that your strategy is to interrupt the anger experience. Even if it is momentary, it helps you de-escalate.

There is one more important point about time-outs: You must take a time-out when you are experiencing low levels of anger—irritation, annoyance, frustration—because these low levels of anger can quickly become full blown. Taking a time-out when you are irritated or annoyed will also give you a headstart in recognizing what provokes you. It is also easier to take a time-out when you are irritated or annoyed than when you are experiencing full-blown anger. If you can't take a time-out at low levels of anger, it is doubtful that you will be able to take one when your anger becomes more intense.

Generating Productive Anger Behavior

If you can stop anger from escalating and rid yourself of anger actions, you are on the verge of making your behavior work for you. To push yourself over the hump you need to fulfill only two more requirements.

First, you must know how to generate new behaviors that will help you resolve the anger-provoking situation.

Second, you must have some tools that will help you actualize your new behaviors; otherwise, nothing will change, old anger actions will emerge, and you will find yourself once again making the situation worse.

Becoming an effective problem solver helps you meet the first requirement. Learning two behavioral change strategies gives you the second.

ANGER AND PROBLEMS

Recall that crucial to anger management is being able to generate the best response to a particular situation. This line of thinking allows us to conceptualize anger management as a problem-solving situation; the task becomes finding the solution that will resolve the anger provocation. What is especially important is that this problem-solving approach makes you proactive in contrast to being reactive—you become responsible for your actions rather than victimized by the situation.

Understanding Problems

The first step is to understand the nature of problems. An essential is to define problems not in terms of impossible situations but in terms of ineffective solutions. Life may be thought of as an endless series of situations that require some kind of response. Looking at it from this point of view, no situation is inherently a problem. It is the ineffectiveness of your response that makes it so.

For example, the fact that you have misplaced an important document and can't find it is not in itself a problem. It becomes a problem only if you neglect to look under the stack of papers on your desk where it is most likely to be found. If you look in your drawers and briefcase or on your car dashboard, you are beginning to create a problem—your response is not effective in finding the misplaced paper. The situation now becomes a problem and begins to provoke you.

Sometimes you turn a situation into a problem by using a response that seems effective at the time but proves to be disastrous in the long run. If you are frequently late to your work station and your co-worker complains about it, you don't necessarily have a problem. You have a problem only if your response is ultimately ineffective. Your solution might be to discourage further comments by exploding whenever your co-worker confronts you. Such a plan would give you good results almost immediately. But over time, your relationship and performance will worsen. Your solution had short-term success but was ineffectual over time. Evaluating the consequences of such false short-term solutions and creating alternative responses that pay off in the long run is part of managing anger effectively.

BECOMING A PROBLEM SOLVER

Problem solving is made easier when you adopt the problem solver's outlook. Based on the principle that an individual's general orientation, or "set," in approaching a situation can greatly influence the way in which he will respond to that situation, the problem solver's outlook encourages independent problem-solving behavior by having you:

- Accept the fact that problems constitute a normal part of life, and that it is possible to cope with most of these situations. This may be obvious, but people are inclined to think that it isn't okay to have problems. We see problems as something to hide as though to acknowledge them was to admit to personal failures. How many times have you heard or thought "I don't want to burden you with my problems"? This is the attitude of the poor problem solver.
- Recognize problems when they occur. Typically, we do not recognize that we have a problem until we find ourselves failing in a situation. In contrast, the able problem solver quickly knows when she is not effective and uses her ineffectiveness as a cue that it is time to change her response.
- Inhibit your tendency to respond either on the first impulse or by doing nothing at all. Ineffective problem solvers tend to be impulsive, impatient, and quick to give up if a solution is not immediately apparent. They then become angry and their problem-solving efforts become more ineffective until they eventually diminish completely, resulting in anger actions.

In contrast, successful problem solvers manage themselves so that they do not respond automatically and inappropriately to problems. Their proactive attitude—"I must take action"—converts their anger arousal into motivation so they can overcome the tendency to do nothing. What do they do? They solve their problems.

SOLVE Your Problems

You will now learn a five-step model that will help you create new solutions to any kind of problem you encounter. The model has two major goals. First, to give you the skills that will make available to you the greatest variety of potentially effective responses for dealing with a provoking situation. The second goal is to increase the probability that you will select the best response from your various options. To help you remember the model, remember the acronym SOLVE:

S   State your problem
O   Outline your response
L   List your alternatives
V   Visualize your consequences
E   Evaluate your results

1. **State your problem**. Define and identify the problem situations in your life. People normally experience problems in areas such as work, finance, health, social relationships, and family life. Thinking about each of these aspects of your life will help identify the area in which you operate least effectively and have the most problems. This is the area you will focus on as you develop your problem-solving skills.

2. **Outline your response**. Specifically and comprehensively describe the problem and your usual response. You must avoid the use of terms that are too vague or ambiguous to be meaningful. Consider all the available facts and information and, if necessary, seek additional information. When you state a problem specifically and concretely, you force yourself to make relevant what might have seemed at first glance to be irrelevant. Research has demonstrated that effective problem solvers typically translate abstract

terms into concrete examples, whereas poor problem solvers usually make no such translation. But one cannot deal directly with an array of facts. When you formulate the various issues reflected in the details of the situation, the direction of the problem-solving process becomes more clearly focused.

Answering these questions will help you make the problem specific:

- Who is involved?
- What does or does not happen that provokes you?
- When does it happen?
- Why does it happen?
- How does it happen?

Focusing on the following points will help you specify your automatic response in terms of what you do or don't do:

- How you do it.
- How you feel.
- Why you do it.
- What you want.

After you have defined your problem in detail, you can look at it in different ways. The technique to use is reframing, changing your perception of the situation so that you can generate novel responses. Some reframing thoughts are:

The real problem isn't who is involved; the real problem is where you respond.

The real problem isn't what's done that bothers you; the real problem is when you respond.

The real problem isn't how it happens; the real problem is how you feel.

The real problem isn't why it happens; the real problem is why
   you respond the way you do.
The real problem isn't the situation; the real problem is how
   you respond.

Some of the sentences you create by reframing your problem
may not make any sense to you. Others may give you penetrating
insights for coming up with an effective solution. The real problem is most likely going to be your response to the situation you
want to change.

When you reframe a problem, you shift the creation of the
problem from the situation to you, thus giving you the power to
deal with the problem by changing your response. You have em-
powered yourself. An additional reason for reframing a problem
is to help you generate some goals that will contribute to your
creating an effective response.

   3.   **List your alternatives.** The task here is to develop possible
        solutions appropriate to the problem situation and to do
        it in such a way that the most effective response will prob-
        ably emerge. A good problem solver will devise at least
        half a dozen strategies for accomplishing each goal. Do
        this through brainstorming, a process of finding ideas.
        There are four basic rules when you brainstorm:

   1.   Destructive criticism is ruled out. Adverse judgments
        about the idea are deferred to a later decision-making
        phase. Just write your idea down.
   2.   Freewheeling is welcomed. The wilder the idea, the better.
        It is easier to tame than to think up.
   3.   Quantity is wanted. The greater the number of ideas, the
        better the likelihood of useful ideas. Don't stop until your
        list is good and long.
   4.   Combination and improvement are sought.

Review your list to see how some of your ideas can be turned into better ones or how two or more ideas could be combined into still another idea. Use productive criticism.

At this point, your brainstorming should be geared to formulating general strategies for appropriate solutions. You need a good plan first. Leave the details for later.

4. **Visualize the consequences.** Now that you have several different goals, each with plans for implementing solutions, you are ready to "visualize" the consequences so that you can select the best solution. Some people do this quickly and automatically; others are slow and make an effort to consciously anticipate what consequences will result. Whether you are automatic or deliberate, this part of the problem solving will be most helpful to do when you do it thoroughly, rigorously, and consciously. Here's how:

- Go over the strategies to your goals, crossing out each one that is clearly ineffective. Be on the lookout for combining one into several. Be oriented to solutions that are long term and/or interpersonally oriented, when applicable.
- Write down the three best strategies. Under each one, list any positive and negative consequences that might result. Helpful questions to ask yourself are: How would this strategy affect what I feel, need, want? How would it affect people in my life? What are its short-term and long-term consequences? Visualize yourself dealing with the different outcomes. Choose the plan that has the best outcomes.

5. **Evaluate your results.** You have now analyzed the demands of the situation, generated the various courses of action, and made a decision on the basis of your rating of the consequences. The final stage is the hardest because

you now have to act. You have a new response to an old situation. It is time to turn your decisions into actions.

After you have tried your new response several times, observe the actual consequences. Are they happening as you thought? Are the results meeting your goal? Is this solution actually better than the old one? If not, use problem solving to develop alternative strategies. You may also want to repeat other parts of the problem-solving process. The successful anger manager does this until she has found a productive action to take.

Changing Your Behavior:
Making New Actions Easier

There will be many times when the only way to manage anger is for you to change your behavior. Having to increase your sales calls, stop being abrasive, get to meetings on time are all common examples of when the way to resolve anger requires you to change. Obviously, change is easier said than done. Weight watchers, smokers, and drinkers can attest to this, as well as the employee who frequently runs behind schedule.

Changing behavior means breaking old habits and giving up attitudes that we have long held. It also means newness, dealing with the unknown. Some people with self-defeating attitudes also think of change as an admission that they are wrong and end up staying the same to prove they are right.

Sometimes change is difficult because we get trapped by our own inertia. Other times, we are overwhelmed by the task at hand, proclaiming that it's too hard. And sometimes we just don't know how to get going, how to take that first step.

Whatever the reason, changing your behavior usually does not happen unless you make a concentrated attempt to steer your efforts toward the results you want. Here are two easy-to-use strategies that will help you change:

Monitor Your Behavior and Visually Graph It

Psychologists have found that monitoring your behavior and visually graphing the results in a particular effort is an extremely effective way of changing your behavior. They give two reasons for its success: 1) The visual data show that you are improving and thus keep you motivated; 2) The act of graphing the behavior is reactive—it forces you to be consciously aware of your actions, which enables you to guide yourself more effectively. It encourages positive self-consciousness. To use this strategy:

1. Specify the behavior you will graph.
2. Determine an accurate measure for the behavior and, when the behavior occurs, measure and record it.
3. Put your results on a graph and keep it in plain sight.

Give Yourself Step-by-Step Tasks and Assignments

Prevent yourself from being overwhelmed by what you have to accomplish. Do this by breaking down into small, manageable tasks and assignments the changes being attempted. As you achieve each one, you gain momentum and your confidence builds for successfully mastering the next task.

Instead of worrying or getting angry about the fact that you have to rewrite a thirty-page proposal (the wasted time and energy prevents you from accomplishing the goal), just focus on rewriting the introduction. Then move on to the next section. After a while, the report will be finished.

Instead of trying to change the entire way you relate to your co-workers, just pick one aspect—criticize more effectively, for example—to get the ball rolling.

The Best Thing to Do Revisited

Recall the section on channeling your arousal. There, the emphasis was on corralling your anger arousal as a means of giving you energy for productive action. Here, the emphasis is on choosing your best response so that you can act productively. The best way to do this is to get in the habit of using the self-statement "What's the best thing to do?" This self-statement will be your guiding force for productive action regardless of the anger-provoking encounter. Common application of this might be:

Going to be late for a meeting? What's the best thing to do?
Your subordinate forgot to give you an important message. What's the best thing to do?
Your boss gives you unrealistic deadlines. What's the best thing to do?

No matter what the situation is, the self-statement will keep you focused on taking a productive action.

All of these change strategies have one thing in common: You must do them to make them work. You must take action.

Key Concepts: How you act when you are angry is influenced by many factors including the learning principles of modeling (learning through observation) and operant learning (learning what to do based on the reaction you get to your response). These principles can be applied to managing anger at work and will demonstrate to others how to manage anger effectively by showing how to motivate and encourage appropriate anger actions in others. Although it seems we always act the same when we are angry, we can learn to act more productively. The key is to view a provocation as a problem with the task being to generate a new response that solves that problem. Once you come up with a novel solution, you need to act on it. This is made easier by visually increasing your awareness of your response pattern and/ or changing your behavior in a series of steps.

Anger in Motion

Here is your chance to assess your anger management knowledge. The following case study illustrates anger in motion—the dynamic process of the different dimensions of anger simultaneously affecting each other. Read the study and then respond to the questions that follow. If you have been doing your reading, it will be a breeze.

THE COFFEE STAIN

Monday Schedule

9:00 to 9:30:	Return Friday's phone calls
9:30 to 10:00:	Progress meeting with assistant on a product-development project
10:00 to 12:00	Staff meeting to discuss budgets, project priorities

Noon to 1:00:   Lunch with prospective buyer for new product
1:30 to 3:30:   Paperwork
3:30 to 4:30:   Meeting with boss to discuss new product de-
                   velopment
4:30 to 5:00:   Meeting with secretary to discuss week's activ-
                   ities
5:00 to 6:00:   Go downtown to pick up theater tickets for you,
                   your wife, and her parents

The Fuse

Monday morning really begins Sunday night. A few minutes before you doze off, your thoughts turn to the new product that has
been in development for six months. Feelings of excitement race
through your body as you remember the day you convinced your
boss to let you run with the ball. Everything has been going great,
and after tomorrow's meeting with your boss, you know that your
promotion is just around the corner. Next Saturday's celebration of
your in-laws' anniversary will be a celebration for you too! Visual-
izing your new office helps put you to sleep.

You don't need the alarm clock to wake up. Although your family
is still sleeping, your adrenaline is already flowing. You dress qui-
etly, go downstairs, and, while you really don't need it, brew a pot
of coffee, pour a cup, and gulp it down. You fail to notice that you
got a tiny drop on the cuff of your shirt.

It's now time to leave. It's pretty early, but you figure you will
beat the traffic and maybe have a doughnut in the building's coffee
shop.

Walking outside your house, you immediately notice that your
wife's car is blocking yours. You can't leave. The thought of being
late to work on such a crucial day flashes through your mind. You
start to appraise the situation as being bad, and the fact your
adrenaline is pumping heightens your focus on this point and prevents you from recognizing that you are still way ahead of sched-

ule. Because you're not thinking clearly, it doesn't occur to you to find the keys and move your wife's car yourself.

You rush back inside and quickly run upstairs to ask your wife to move her car. As you go upstairs, you think about how thoughtless it was for her to block your car. "She should have known," you tell yourself. Into the bedroom you go. You loudly whisper, "Wake up. Hurry. Move your car! You blocked me in. You know I have a big meeting today. I can't believe you did this. Just put your robe on."

Your spouse asks you to be quiet. It's very early and the kids do not have to get up for school yet. You immediately respond by telling her again to hurry up. You cannot afford to be late. She's always doing things like this and pays no attention to what is important to you.

As she goes downstairs to move her car, you follow her, continually reminding her that this is just like the time she forgot to pick up your clothes at the cleaners.

Your wife moves the car and, just as you are pulling out of the driveway, she yells out, "Have a good day." You give her a harsh look, happy that you are finally on your way, but not feeling great.

Your spouse, catching the look, begins to feel bad. Angry too. In fact, she is soon telling herself that you are always jumping on her. She goes upstairs and loudly tells the kids, "Get dressed and hurry up or you will be late to school."

The Bomb

You arrive at work and you can't believe it: Construction has started in the company parking lot! "What a disaster," you tell yourself. A sign tells you to make two lefts and a right and another left to park. You realize that you'd better hurry or you will not be able to return all your phone calls. This thought holds your attention so that you inadvertently miss the second left and end up in an unfamiliar side street. You begin to sweat.

You drive to the end of the block and immediately ask a person standing on the corner how to get to the closest parking lot. He doesn't know. You drive around for what seems to be an eternity but is really only two or three minutes. You find a parking space, grab your briefcase, and walk briskly to your office building.

Entering the building, you see that you are still thirty minutes ahead of schedule. To help you relax, you pick up a cup of coffee and a chocolate doughnut.

Getting into the elevator, you see your boss. You and a few other early birds ride up to your floor together. You are surprised that your boss does not say anything about how he is looking forward to this afternoon's meeting. You also note that he doesn't look happy and that he is not looking at you. You ask yourself what's wrong and make the appraisal that he is not happy with your project and will be telling you that this afternoon. You get off the elevator feeling terrible. Stopping by your secretary's desk, you tell her not to put any calls through. Feeling a little down, you give her the doughnut but keep the coffee.

Sitting behind the desk, you think about how you have blown this opportunity. The possibility of actually getting fired now seems possible, plus you failed to return one of your important messages from Friday. Your stomach gets a little queasy with fear. Before you know it, your assistant appears.

Although your assistant is excited about the upcoming meeting, she is immediately met by a frown on your face. She becomes slightly less enthused. Not wanting to rock the boat, you tell her in a very businesslike tone that everything is fine and ask her for an update.

She tells you that she and her team are coming up with new data and new ideas about the product that she believes will significantly increase its quality and profit. These new developments will, however, require about three additional months to integrate into the current product design.

"Three months!" you hear yourself say. No wonder your boss was upset. "Three months would put us behind schedule. Over budget too. My boss will flip. Forget about my promotion." These thoughts dominate your thinking, preventing you from tuning in to your assistant's analysis that the project would still come in on budget and be much more profitable than ever imagined. You tell her that three months is out of the question. The plan is to keep the product the same.

Your assistant is surprised. She cannot understand how you could not go along with this breakthrough. She asks for an elaboration of the decision. Your response is vague and when she presses for more information, you tell her to stop being defensive. You direct her to tell the team that the product stays the same. She leaves infected with your mood.

Ten minutes before the staff meeting you note your memo about picking up theater tickets. "How much are they?" you ask yourself. "Sixty-five bucks each! Jeez!"

Before going into the staff meeting, you take two Tylenols for a headache that seemed to come out of nowhere.

You wonder if your boss will say anything to you. A few minutes later, a colleague enters the conference room and tells all that your boss will not be able to attend the meeting. Could he be avoiding you?

The staff meeting lasts two hours. It seems to drag on forever. You spend the first hour thinking about how hard you worked to get this opportunity and that you have blown it big time. You start to feel depressed, knowing that it will be a long, long time before you get another assignment with so much responsibility. A promotion is out of the question.

For the second hour of the meeting, you think about your spouse, your assistant, and your secretary. All of them have been screwing up lately.

A colleague's question interrupts your thinking, so you have to ask him to repeat it. When he does, your response carries no weight, which is not surprising considering that you were not listening to the details of the previous hour and a half.

The meeting adjourns and you are the first to leave. Several of your co-workers ask if there is anything wrong with you.

You now realize that you have a few minutes before meeting with your client in the building's restaurant. As you are walking to your office, you pass your boss's secretary, who tells you that your boss has asked if he can move your meeting up to 1 P.M. Although this creates a problem for you with your lunch meeting, you tells her, "No problemo." You are now sure that there is a major problem.

Your client is a few minutes late but is very happy to see you. Small talk goes for just a few minutes, as you want to be out of there by quarter of so you will not keep your boss waiting.

Your client tells you that she is very excited about your product and that her company expects to order a large volume. She asks how it is coming. You are afraid to tell her the truth so you report that everything is great. That being the case, she tells you that she will be giving the product description to her catalogs for the fall season. You figure you will call her in a few days to give her the bad news, which will be better than telling her right now.

You've ordered light, and as you reach for the salad dressing, you see the coffee stain on your shirt cuff. You look at your client to see if she notices. You think she does. Nevertheless, your boss is sure to, and that doesn't help your image. You immediately decide to tell the cleaner that he'd better be more careful.

Although your client seems to be taken aback with your need to end lunch so soon, you fail to notice. You pay the check and tell her you will call her in a few days. She nods but is a little bewildered.

Stopping in the bathroom, you realize you are perspiring, and the coffee stain seems to be much bigger now. Your wife should have seen it when she picked up the cleaning.

You walk anxiously down the hall, ignoring those you pass. At your boss's office, his secretary tells you, "You are a few minutes early; he's on the phone. Just have a seat." "How are things going?" you ask, trying to see if you can learn something. "So-so" is the reply, which doesn't make you feel better.

The door opens and your boss tells you to come in. No small talk. He asks for an update. You immediately tell him that you have been working on the product and you are very confident that it is going to be a big success. You tell him it is on schedule and that you will bring it in on budget. You have his attention so you give him more details.

He asks if the product is the same as originally planned. You assure him it is. Before he continues, his secretary interrupts to tell him he has an important call. He takes it with you thinking how rude he is and that if you were to take a call in his presence, you would be sure to lose points.

He stays on for less than a minute. He then continues by saying he has heard about some recent developments in your product area that if integrated into your product could have a significant positive impact on the bottom line. He doesn't know the specifics, but the two of you will have to sit down to talk things through. As he gently ushers you out of his office, he suggests that you get caught up on these new developments and do your homework before the next meeting so you can brief him.

You walk out feeling really stupid. Your thoughts are punching. "I looked like a jerk and I came across like I didn't know anything." You now know your performance appraisal will be terrible. "No way am I getting a promotion. No raise."

Walking back to your office, you think about the meeting you had with your assistant. You realize that she and your boss are probably talking about the same research developments. Although you admit that your assistant tried to explain these items to you, you conclude that she should have sent you a memo so that you would be up to date. "It's her fault. If she had done that, everything would have been okay." When you reach your office, you tell your secretary to summon your assistant.

She arrives, and because of your earlier meeting, your moods match. Tension is in the air. You tell her that there have been recent developments in the product line that could greatly impact the bottom line. You ask her if she is aware of this, but before she opens her mouth, you tell her that she should have sent you a memo detailing all these factors.

She is shocked. Raising her voice, she tells you she tried to explain them to you this morning and that she had called you on Friday to arrange a precall before your morning meeting so you would have known what to expect.

Shaking your head, you again tell her she should have put it in writing. Your voice is rising too. You go on to point out that a few weeks ago, she was late to an important meeting and that you cannot have this type of irresponsibility. You dismiss her by ordering a full report about these new product changes and demand that you have it before the week is over. In the next breath, you tell her that your secretary will contact her for her performance appraisal. With thick sarcasm, she says, "I'm really looking forward to it."

She leaves, and you feel a little better knowing that you have straightened her out. Your thoughts now turn back to your boss's meeting. "He was so short with me. He obviously doesn't think I can handle this project. I'm not going to make it."

Despite the important paperwork on your desk, you cannot motivate yourself. You tell your secretary that you will meet with her tomorrow. The day passes, and before you know it, 5 P.M. comes around. You've accomplished nothing.

Walking to your car, you remember that you have to pick up theater tickets. Your dialogue is: "How much are they? Sixty-five bucks each! No way. Not now. I can't afford it. When was the last time my in-laws got me a nice gift? What did they give us, a bunch of trays, for our anniversary. Forget it. I'll order a pizza for them. My wife will have to understand that we cannot afford to spend this money now."

As you get into your car and grab the steering wheel, you can't help but notice the coffee stain. It's huge. "God, I looked like a slob all day. My client probably noticed too. Now I have to call her to tell her that the product is on hold. Another disaster for my reputation."

Fighting the traffic, you look forward to getting home so you can confront your spouse about her thoughtlessness. "How could she block me in? She should have gotten up with me. She can't even get me a clean shirt." Your headache is worse.

The Explosion

Pulling into your driveway, you note your kids' bikes and bike helmets lying on the grass. "They never take care of anything." You think the bike helmets look new and quickly calculate that they cost about a hundred bucks. They are not getting anything new for two months, you decide.

You enter your home and walk into the kitchen. Your wife is on the phone and you motion for her to get off. She ignores you but soon ends her conversation by saying how great the play is going to be. Another long-distance call. She hangs up and asks, "What's up?"

You begin your attack. First, you tell her that you are really upset. That it was terrible what she did to you this morning. How could she park you in on such an important day? She starts to respond, but you raise your voice and tell her to be quiet and just listen. "You always do this."

You tell your wife that your client thought you looked like a slob. You had a big coffee stain on your shirt, and she'd better go back to the cleaners immediately to demand a new shirt because they ruined this one. How could she, you ask, not make sure that you had a good shirt to wear?

Your wife says she is sorry, but you tell her to forget it. You think she is just like your assistant. "She never listens."

Your wife defends herself and says you are blowing things way out of proportion.

"See," you say. "You never think anything I say is important. All you think of is yourself."

Your spouse tries to change the subject.

"I can't *wait* to see the play."

"*Play!*" you scream. "You must be *crazy*. How can you think we can afford to go to that play? Plus, your parents never do anything nice for us. I'll give them a pizza."

Your wife becomes visibly upset. "What do you *mean* no play! Didn't you get the tickets?"

You tell her that you have a lot of expenses and that you cannot afford theater tickets and that is final.

She is angry. She points out that you have planned on seeing this play for several months. The money has already been budgeted. There is no reason not to go. It will be fun, and her parents are counting on it.

You respond that you could care less what her parents are expecting. No play. It's final.

Your kids enter the kitchen. Before they say anything, you blast them for not putting their bike helmets away and tell them that if they can't take care of them, you'll give the helmets to kids who *can* appreciate them. You order them to do it right this minute.

Back to your wife. She approaches you and asks what is really wrong. You tell her that you don't want to talk about it anymore. She says, "You never want to talk about things. All you do is yell and scream. It's too much."

"Fine," you yell. "Then *leave!*"

The kids come back into the kitchen. You immediately yell out, "We are getting a divorce."

Both kids are shocked. They begin to cry and run to their rooms. You hear the doors slam. Your wife starts to cry. Your headache throbs.

"I'm getting out of here."

You get back into your car, drive to a bar, and have a drink. You think about how bad things are for you.

A few hours later, you return home. Your kids are sleeping, but your wife is waiting up for you. You acknowledge her presence, tell her that you have a big day tomorrow and that you are going to sleep. She soon follows you up.

You sleep on opposite sides of the bed. Your last thoughts are how terrible things are going to be tomorrow.

The Fallout

The next morning everybody keeps to himself. At breakfast, you announce that you have a lot of work to do and will be home late. You excuse yourself and leave, happy to get out of a tense situation but feeling down by the time you get to work.

Your wife tells your kids to take the bus home, goes into the bedroom, and shuts the door.

The kids hear their mother talking to her sister about all her unhappiness.

The kids go to school scared.

Test Questions

1. How did self-awareness influence the anger experience?

2a. Give some examples of how the cognitive dimension affected the anger experience. Think about appraisals, self-statements, distorted thinking styles, and expectations.

2b. Where and how could you have used some cognitive interventions, especially with the boss?

3. Where was anger arousal a factor? How was it made worse?

4. Where did emotional contagion operate? What were the mechanisms of mood transmission? When could you have used some emotional arousal anger management interventions?

5.	What could your wife have done differently to prevent the explosion? What behavioral interventions could she have tried? How might your wife respond to your anger more effectively?

6.	How could you have used mood information in dealing more effectively with your boss?

7.	Where was it important to use the feeling dimension effectively?

8.	How could the fallout have been handled productively? What dimensions do you think would be most important?

Extra Credit

1.	As you read "The Coffee Stain," how were you feeling? What physical sensations, if any, did you note?

2.	What parts did you relate to personally?

3.	What anger management interventions do you think would be most useful?

If you have no difficulty explaining and elaborating on your answers, you are an A student and ready to develop the art of anger management.

If you find it difficult to explain your answers, then I recommend you review the material until you can pass the test with flying colors.

The Art of
Anger
Management

The focus of this section is two-fold: first, to delineate a general framework of how to handle anger on the job and, second, to illustrate how to apply a wide range of anger management principles and interventions in the context of work.

I will assume that you have digested the foregoing material and have become well familiarized with the different dimensions of anger. This is crucial if you are to become proficient in the art of anger management. When you master this art, you will be using anger as a powerful tool to enhance your productivity in multiple ways. It will also help minimize your chances of encountering barriers to productivity that range from conflict with co-workers to self-defeating outbursts.

Anger on the Job: A General Framework

Although it is true that different provocations require different anger management interventions, there are a few generics that must be applied to all provocations if you are to manage them effectively. These generics provide us with a general framework for managing anger on the job. You will note that, depending on the step to take, some dimensions of anger are more prevalent than others.

STEP 1: VALIDATE AND ACKNOWLEDGE YOUR ANGER

The first step in managing anger on the job is to validate that you are angry by admitting it to yourself. Anger that we validate is much less harmful than unrecognized or unadmitted anger. Self-awareness is, therefore, of immediate importance.

To be sure, there are times when you instantly recognize your anger (when you have an outburst, slam down the phone, or walk out of a meeting). For these "impossible not to acknowledge anger moments," Step 2 becomes your first task. There are many other times, though, when we are angry and fail to see it. This anger becomes deadly because by going undetected, it becomes unmanageable, inevitably affecting your performance, your relationships, and your health.

The point to note is that acknowledging you are angry is more than just cognitive awareness; it is also feeling awareness. In other words, until you allow yourself to feel the anger, you will not be able to manage it effectively. Validating the anger is feeling the anger, and sometimes feeling the anger is so threatening to the individual that he cannot do it without professional help.

Why do we fail to acknowledge our anger? Recall the section on stuffing feelings. People will continue to speak of being disappointed, annoyed, frustrated, let down, unaware that these expressions may indicate stuffed anger. Emotions and feelings are stuffed because they are unacceptable. Anger may be denied because we feel too guilty about it or are afraid of it, and these feelings may be beyond our awareness.

What to do? Focus on your immediate feelings, which give you clues that you are stuffing anger. If you are tense and talking about being frustrated, disappointed, or—more obviously—ready to explode, or if you are using any of the other expressions that hint at hidden anger, ask yourself, "Am I angry about something? What is it? Am I afraid to face the situation? Am I afraid to face the anger?" Until you can acknowledge the anger, you cannot decide what to do about it. Meanwhile, the anger will continue to eat at you.

It is also important to be aware that feelings of guilt or of unreasonableness must not deter you from looking for the clue. Just because anger is not rational does not mean it does not exist. If the guilt or the sense that the anger is unjustified makes you pass judgment on these feelings, you will not get beyond this first step.

Remember, anger has many dimensions. To be aware of it purely cognitively is not more than one fifth of the way to truly recognizing it. This is why feeling talk is so important: It helps you express your feelings of anger, thereby giving you a means for validating it. Once you can feel the anger and accept the fact that you are angry, you can move on to the next step.

Step 2: Manage the Anger Arousal Immediately

Showing inappropriate emotional arousal on the job is undesirable. It makes you look out of control, impedes your work, and impairs your health. Therefore, you must manage the arousal immediately. Your tool kit for this job includes using anger management instructions, counterpunching, relaxation response, time-out, and any other interventions you have discovered that allow you to calm yourself to a level of composure.

You will be most effective when you can manage your anger arousal by converting it into energy. Do this by turning your attention to job activities that have to get done. If you are too angry to sit down and be creative, use your anger arousal to do your busywork so at least you are getting something accomplished. You feel productive and regain a sense of control so that you can go back to productively confront the source of your anger.

A helpful tip is to write down a bunch of tasks you know you can do when you are angry; this will make it easier for you to know what to do when you are angry. I have found that knowing what to do when you are angry is a good antidote to being immobilized by anger on the job.

STEP 3: IDENTIFY THE PROVOCATION

We have already talked about the importance of identifying provocations, and you may want to do a quick review of that section. Key to remember is that different provocations require different anger management interventions. The frustration of a broken copy machine may be handled by your self-statements and alerting the proper person so it can be fixed. The anger provoked by an abrasive employee may require you to use some confrontation and criticism skills.

Since anger is frequently not reasonable (as in the case of cognitive distortions), it is critical that when you do identify the provocation, you immediately begin to explore your appraisals and self-statements for cognitive distortions, as this will often help you nip anger in the bud.

In many instances, it is very easy to identify the provocation. If someone intentionally embarrasses you, you don't have to look very far to find the source of your anger. If, however, a team member inadvertently says something that embarrasses you, the anger may seem less reasonable (she didn't do it on purpose; she didn't know it would embarrass you) but the cause is still pretty clear.

However, sometimes the provocation or source of your anger may be difficult to flesh out if the real instigator of the anger is someone who is powerful or who can harm you in some way and with whom it is not, therefore, prudent to be angry. What do you do?

You already know that many people handle their anger by stuffing it. It is also common practice to handle anger by looking for another possible source on which to blame the anger. This is known as displacement, and when and why we do it is usually beyond our awareness. You may, for example, be angry at your client for his frequent last-minute cancellations but instead say you are angry with your kids because they are not doing their chores at home. You may feel that expressing anger at your client threatens your business, so you growl at your kids for not making their beds.

Another widespread reason for displacing anger is to avoid humiliating or belittling yourself. It's easier to blame your secretary for your showing up at the wrong time, when, in fact, only you knew about the appointment.

Guilt can also confuse the real source of anger. Many managers and supervisors believe they are not supposed to get angry at their subordinates. So when they get home, they blast their spouses for not having dinner ready. An often experienced variation of this is the "road to anger is paved with good intentions" syndrome. For example, a tax attorney strongly recommends that your company create a manufacturing plant in another state to reduce taxes. The company builds the plant and the law is changed. How can you be angry with the attorney, who meant only to save money for your company? Still, you are furious, but you are in a bind because his intentions were the best. This is one of the most difficult sources of anger for people to handle. Many a manager and parent has said, "They try their best. How can I get angry?" But the anger still remains.

A good clue to displacement is anger that is out of proportion to the cause. Then you must suspect that the situation is an outlet for anger generated by someone or something else, but because of fear or guilt that anger must be denied.

STEP 4: EMPOWER YOURSELF—ACKNOWLEDGE THAT YOU ARE CHOOSING TO KEEP YOUR JOB

When angry on the job, people often tell themselves, "That's the way it is; there's nothing I can do about it." "I have to accept it." "It's not that terrible." While these anger management statements help you initially to release your anger, they do not help you effectively manage it because they also imply that you are helpless—a thought and feeling that provoke anger, not reduce it. Chronic anger may result.

It is much better to realize that you don't have to accept it; in truth, you can leave, you can always quit. However, quitting is usually not a realistic option. Most of us need to work simply for economic reasons, and if we don't, the fact still remains that working is essential to good mental health. You are much better off acknowledging that you don't want to leave; you want to keep your job.

This thinking helps you in at least two ways. First, it allows you to validate that you're angry but helps you keep the perspective that anger comes with the territory. Remember, work is naturally provoking. By acknowledging your feelings, you will not be stuffing them in a dysfunctional manner. You may still wish to conceal your anger but your choice is based on political reasons rather than psychological disturbance. At the very least, your acknowledgment brings anger into awareness.

Second, recognizing that you are angry but want to keep your job puts you back in control. While the situation is unpleasant, the fact is it is your choice to remain. You can become an effective anger manager by adopting the attitude: "Given the fact that I'm angry and I want to keep my job, what can I do about it so it doesn't happen again?" This attitude provides the impetus for turning your anger arousal into energy so that you can develop an effective anger management intervention.

STEP 5: CHOOSE YOUR BEST RESPONSE

You know you're angry; you know what is provoking you. Your next step is to choose your best response to the situation. Remember to use SOLVE.

Make it easier by reflecting more on the reasons you are angry. Is it because your feelings have been hurt or because you feel there is an unjust situation? Maybe you're angry because you are not getting the recognition you deserve. Or could it be that you are provoked by your client's behavior of always being late to meetings? The more you know about your anger and the reasons why you are provoked, the more adept you will become at choosing your best response.

These five steps—acknowledging anger, managing anger arousal, identifying the provocation, empowering yourself, and choosing the best response—comprise the generic model for managing anger on the job. Now it is time to illustrate the model in action with emphasis on choosing your best response.

Anger on the Job: Specifics

I will illustrate concrete, creative, and practical applications of anger management concepts in the context of The Dirty Dozen—situations that are described as being intensely anger provoking and extremely difficult to handle. These situations provoke anger because they threaten needs, are abusive in nature, or reflect an injustice.

The situations have been identified by surveys with a sample size of more than seven thousand working people who represent CEOs, executives, middle managers, clerical staff, line employees, teachers, principals, school administrators, Secret Service, FBI, and CIA agents, bankers and lawyers, athletes and actors, air-traffic controllers, emergency room nurses, and dozens of other occupations.

Here are The Dirty Dozen with emphasis on choosing your best anger management response.

THE DIRTY DOZEN

1. **General harassment.** Whether it's sexual harassment or harassment in the form of the boss who is always on your back for producing less than quality work but never tells you ways to improve, harassment provokes anger because it is abuse. Your anger will help you protect you if you put it to use to assert and confront.

Being assertive will communicate how you feel about the situation, and your productive confrontation will call for stopping the harassing behavior. If this doesn't work—the harasser may deny his behavior—you will have to take a different route. For example, if it's a boss who demands perfection but never gives you the how-tos and always finds fault with whatever you do, you might find it effective to tell him that you are doing the best you can unless he can tell you specific ways to improve. To ensure that this does not escalate the situation, don't sound defensive or disrespectful. Temper your statement by explaining that you value his opinion and want his input. The process will help clarify expectations—on his part.

If it's sexual harassment, follow your corporate guidelines. Remember, the law is on your side.

A thought to remember is that when you deal with any type of harassment, the traps to avoid are the fear of repercussions and feelings of guilt. Fear and guilt feelings will keep you in the victim role, inevitably creating feelings of helplessness, despair, and even depression. Don't be afraid of your anger. Here it is signaling that you are being abused, and it is simply arousing you to give you the energy to confront the harasser.

2. **Favoritism.** Equity theory tells us people get angry when they don't get what they perceive to be fair, whether it's a promotion, pay raise, specific assignment, or parking space. Yet it is

terribly naïve to think that any organization will be without favoritism. There are several ways to manage anger provoked by this injustice. Here are two strategies.

First, restore a sense of equity to the situation. Be very criteria oriented—operationalize, or set goals for, good performance as much as possible. Find out specifically what you have to do to get the promotion, perk, etc., and get agreement that if you do perform to these standards, you will get what you deserve. Your goal is to have enough data to show that you deserve the same rewards as others. If you *don't* get those rewards despite the fact that your behavior and accomplishments match those of others, you know that favoritism is occurring and can force a confrontation. This is okay as long as you are willing to handle the politics (e.g., possible dismissal) of such an outcome.

Although the preceding intervention is the conventional strategy, I find a second course of action to be more effective and an even more realistic response.

I recommend that you try to take advantage of favoritism by becoming the favorite. Align yourself with the power people. Remember positive affect. Put others in a good mood and give them good feelings, which they will associate with you. As already mentioned, these positive feelings tend to carry over into being treated better. Since there will always be favoritism, take advantage of it or be victimized by it.

3. Insensitivity. Not feeling that your needs are being attended to seems to provoke anger in any well-functioning human being. Individuals report many daily examples of how their needs are not met: when organizations do not provide child-care facilities, being forced to take an unwanted job transfer, and not being able to leave work for crucial errands.

Nevertheless, don't waste time and effort trying to turn a corporate culture from being insensitive to sensitive—you can't unless you're the CEO. What you *can* do is develop relationships with those who can help you with specific needs as they arise.

Don't make it a question of righteousness: Should your boss or company allow you to take time off from your work to go to a teacher's conference or a dental appointment? Looking at this issue from a right-wrong perspective will only create conflict and anger, with your boss and company destined to win the fight. The real solution is to check these issues out before you get the position or to clarify expectations before they come up. This way you learn what the rules are and will experience less anger when rules are invoked.

4. Depersonalization. A prevalent feeling in the contemporary working world is that of feeling alone, isolated, disconnected. More to the point, feeling that you don't count, that it is only a job. This is depersonalization, and its end result is a loss of identity to the point that work is experienced as lacking in purpose.

At the root of depersonalization are feelings that you are operating superficially—going through the motions. What is needed is for you to deepen the level of how you relate to others with the goal being to establish more genuine relationships, ones in which you feel safe to communicate in a more intimate manner, be it your aspirations at work or anxieties about a job change. In essence, you must go beyond communicating with your co-workers on a passing level to a deeper level of exchange, one that involves thoughts, feelings, and ideas. Here are some ways to get started:

- Use feeling talk in your everyday conversation.
- Build a support system.
- Get involved in extracurricular corporate activities that are enjoyable.
- Assert yourself to get assignments that are meaningful.

Again, the key is to restore feelings of connectedness by relating to your co-workers with a deeper level of communication.

5. Unfair performance appraisals (UPAs). One of the most important rituals in the working world is performance appraisal.

Promotions, assignments, pay raises, one's future are all affected by this corporate ritual. It is no wonder that unfair performance appraisals provoke even the most timid employee.

UPAs are frequently cited by employees and come in many forms, including those that are inaccurate, not on time, or given but not discussed with you. A confounding problem is that unfair performance appraisals have almost become acceptable in most organizations. The offending manager, therefore, is never held responsible. How could you *not* be angry?

Nevertheless, I've noted that most managers are like umpires—they will rarely change their call. Unless you are prepared to fight until the end, your best choice is to accept the UPA and then concentrate on not allowing it to happen again. Here is a workable plan to achieve fairer appraisals:

Specify what aspects of your performance are going to be appraised and make sure they are prioritized. Also, to clarify criteria, make sure you and your boss know what good performance looks like. If you have to, ask for models of good performance.

Next, increase communication between you and the appraiser. The purpose of this is to continually make sure that you are on the right track. You may find it helpful to request miniappraisals each month. Ask your boss, "If you were giving me my PA now, what would I receive?" Find out why. What is he perceiving? What data are being used? How does he interpret them? Your investigation will serve to help you both align your perceptions and increase the accuracy of the appraisal. It also provides you the opportunity to make changes before the actual appraisal.

If your boss says that you're doing great with no details, quickly ask him if you can assume you will get a perfect rating. When he says no, he is apt to realize that to be fair, he needs to help you by at least giving you some specifics.

You can restore a sense of fairness to a PA with these steps, but you should also remember that the nature of a PA is to be unfair to some people, usually to those who don't think they got what they deserved.

During the PA, use your listening skills so you can hear the reasons your superior is giving you for your rating. Clarify your own expectations and perceptions—perhaps they were distorted. Many times, you leave rethinking your own evaluation and you realize the PA was fair—you just didn't like it.

6. Lack of resources. Lack of resources provokes feelings of helplessness, frustration, and ultimately full-blown anger. First, being asked to do something without adequate support is seen as being unjust. Second, it threatens job achievement. But the bottom line: This is reality and you still have to get the job done. How?

You must act more wisely. Whatever you are doing, do it differently. Use SOLVE. Instead of defining the problem as a lack of resources, see the problem as your response. This will be the catalyst for managing differently.

Who are the gatekeepers to the resources you need? Develop relationships with them. Perhaps they can use their influence to help you out. Prioritize your responsibilities. This act will help you confront your boss about her unrealistic expectations. If she denies she is being unrealistic, ask her for guidance. See if you can get her to explain how the job is to be done given the resources you have. If she says, "That's your job," don't get defensive. Respond with "I'm doing the best I can. I need your help to make this work." Your goal is to get her to either allocate the resources you need—help you manage the situation—or, at the very least, come up with realistic expectations.

Many times, lack of adequate resources will create a company nightmare—interdepartmental conflict. One effective strategy to be used in this scenario is for the manager to set joint goals that serve to unite subgroups. For example, a rift between the marketing and sales departments may be soothed if the manager reminds each department that they are on the same team; their opposition is another company, not each other.

It may also be that there will always be interdepartmental conflict. Here, the goal will be to prevent the conflict from escalating, not total resolution. Individuals skilled in negotiation and mediation strategies will have an edge.

7.   **Lack of adequate training.** It is very frustrating to be asked and expected to be able to perform a task when you have not been sufficiently trained. It prevents you from meeting your goals and it makes you vulnerable to a poor performance appraisal. To manage the anger provoked by this, you need to make some decisions. First, though, realize that the best strategy is to prevent this from happening. Don't put yourself in a position you are inadequately prepared for unless, of course, it is known to everyone that you are learning as you go or you believe the challenge of the opportunity must be taken even if you are ill prepared.

If you find yourself having to perform a job for which you are not amply trained, you can:

- Directly ask for formal training. If you are refused, point out that despite your best intentions, disaster may be looming. By addressing failure, you put yourself in charge rather than dealing with it after the fact, in which case you will be blamed. Also, by directly asking and documenting your request for formal training, you minimize the chances of being blamed at performance appraisal time.
- Seek out informal training. Who can teach you what you need to know? Develop a relationship with these job mentors. Be nice to them, and the positive affect may motivate them to help you out.
- Publicly ask for help. Contrary to the conventional wisdom that says asking for help is weakness, those who ask for help usually outperform those who try to go it alone. By publicly acknowledging that you need help—at staff meetings, for example—you also put your colleagues in the position of being unable to blame you after the fact since all knew you were not adequately trained. Often, asking for help publicly will result in your direct formal request's being granted.

- Take seminars, read books, buy software, etc. There are optional, after-work ways of getting training.
- Finally, continually clarify expectations to remind the power people what your capabilities are for the particular task at hand. In essence, it is probably good policy to expect not to be adequately trained for many of the tasks thrown your way. Rather than take a passive response, which will inevitably lead to anger from you or from those around you, you are better off empowering yourself by taking responsibility to get trained rather than waiting to be trained.

8.   **Lack of teamwork.** Besides impeding work performance for everyone, a lack of teamwork also provokes anger because it prevents individuals from meeting an important psychological need—the need to belong, to feel part of a group, the need to affiliate.

Since you can't have a team of one, your best anger management strategy will be to get others to join the team. Take actions to build cooperative relationships, an underlying dynamic of team building. Again, remember positive affect. Make people feel good so they want to join the team.

You can also build cooperative relationships with a "foot in the door" technique. This is implemented by asking for small favors that you know your co-worker is likely to grant. When he does, be sure to thank him. As you periodically ask for these small favors—and return them too—you will probably get a cooperative momentum going, making it easier to get the big favors you really need for effective team functioning.

Continually emphasize a goal that puts people in the same boat going in the same direction. Passion is important here so that the goal will seem meaningful and exciting.

Point out how your work affects others and vice versa. This breaks down boundaries of competitiveness and gives co-workers permission to give input about colleagues' performance.

If you cannot build cooperative relationships, you may find it effective to confront the group about the lack of teamwork and specifically spell out the negative consequences that are sure to follow if "we don't get our act together pronto."

9.   **Withdrawal of earned benefits.** Plato said two thousand years ago, writing in *The Republic*, "People get angry when they don't receive their entitlements." The common perception is that an injustice has been performed. But has it?

Don't take it personally. You lose health benefits or other perks because your company can't afford to pay for them. Use a cognitive shift—what would you do if you were the CEO, give great benefits while you were losing millions?

An unfortunate reality is that in some cases benefits that are earned *are* taken away. Your best bet is to channel your anger productively. Check to see if benefits are gone forever or if they can be returned. Under what conditions? If possible, work with your colleagues to create those conditions on the grounds that it will return benefits. It may be if your department or company increases revenues by 10 percent you can have lost benefits back. This has been a widely accepted resolution by management and unions across industry.

If the benefit is gone forever, put your anger into determining what your other options are. If, for example, it's a reduction in health benefits, perhaps your spouse's job has a plan or maybe there are other associations through which you can get a plan. For smaller things like no more free sandwiches, either bring your own or continually remind yourself that expenses are being cut. Also, use an alternative explanation—the company is helping you lose weight!

10.   **Lack or violation of trust.** I agree with the position that trust is the cornerstone of a productive relationship, and when it is violated, anger is a just response to the sense of betrayal we experience. But how much trust do you really need or expect in a work environment? A wife can't testify against her husband, but a co-worker sure can.

Your best strategy for dealing with anger provoked by a lack of trust is to clarify your expectations. State your definition of trust. You might find that your definition is actually unrealistic in the context of business. Modify it and do what you need to do to close the gap between what you have and what you want. An important point to remember here is that your business relationships are artificial to the extent that you have not chosen them, as you choose a friend or spouse. Therefore, it is probably wise to bear in mind that there are degrees of trust in business, because, in the end, one's self-interest will usually take precedence over another's. In relationships outside of business, this is not necessarily the case, especially in highly trusting relationships. Nevertheless, it is still helpful to have some people at work whom you can trust. At the very least, trusting relationships are a good antidote to depersonalization.

One avenue to developing trusting relationships is to act in ways that show others they can trust you. Be consistent. Don't withhold information. Give people what they deserve, whether it is an outstanding performance appraisal or a poor one. If something is told to you in confidence and you are pressed to reveal it, say you know but have been instructed to say nothing. This is much better than a blank: "I haven't heard anything." Use your own discretion to give subtle messages that tell others what they want to know. Instead of "I haven't heard anything about layoffs" (you really have but have been told not to say anything), you may want to say, "I have heard some things, but I've been asked not to talk about it. I will tell you, though, that I think it is the smart person who prepares for the worst and knows her options."

In cases when your trust has been violated, you have options. While it may be effective in managing your anger to assert yourself and confront the trust violator, you may find it politically wise to simply bite the bullet and not assume in the future that the person you confided in is trustworthy.

11. Poor communication. Poor communication is an anger provoker because it inevitably prevents you from relating effectively to those around you. What is particularly alarming is that once poor communication is put in motion, it is extremely difficult to stop because it intensifies many of the other provocations.

The first task in managing the anger provoked here is to assess exactly what "poor communication" means. Define it for yourself, the particular situation, and your organization, and you can begin to intervene. Obviously, the goal is to have good communication, but unless you are specific, this means nothing.

For example, good communication may be a manager's ability to communicate criticism productively to her subordinate or it may mean two team members can negotiate a time frame acceptable to both. Poor communication may be a union's perception that it is not being heard by management, or it may also be that the boss rarely articulates his expectations to his staff.

Remember, when you generalize from the specific to the global, you defuse the provocation and it becomes impossible to manage it. When this happens there is a lot of blame, which intensifies the anger (e.g., destructive labeling). Thus, an underlying problem of poor communication is that we define it globally. Giving details helps you figure out a specific strategy to resolve the situation. If criticism is a problem, you can have a training program on the subject or learn on your own how to give it and take it. If it's miscommunication between boss and staff, weekly communication meetings can be built into the system. Do not let poor communication become a blanket for many other problems, as couples often do in therapy.

12. Dallying boss. While it may seem that the dallying boss is an altruistic community-serving member, his behavior provokes anger in the rest of the group, who are trying to take care of business and will be judged on how they perform, not on how they contribute to the community. While too much dallying makes the boss unavailable, the subordinate is still held responsible for meeting his standards and making the right decisions, some of which require the boss's frequent input.

No doubt, then, it is frustrating that your boss is doing things that seem non–job related, but so what? Most people do—from balancing their checkbooks to doing freelance work on company time. Your only concern here is that your boss's dallying does not affect your effectiveness. Since you cannot tell your boss what to do, your best response choice is to try to keep your boss on target in the context of your own goals. Keep him informed about projects so he will be able to use this information to modify his own habits. If he notices that projects are way behind, perhaps he will conclude he needs to dally less.

Tell him when you encounter difficulties and request his help. Most managers will put their dallying on hold to help you.

If dallying continues, you may want to use a communication intervention. Ask him, "Boss, would it be okay if I go to the Boy Scouts lunch? I contribute some time like you do when you go to the United Way events every other Monday." He may either get the message that you are very aware of how he spends his time and that he is away from work too much, or he may say sure. If the latter happens, at least you get to dally too. Too risky? Then don't do it.

Other feelings tend to be operative here too, and one is envy of the person who can overtly do other things that are not job related. When these things are perceived as challenging, exciting, fun, sure we get angry, because we want do be able to do the same. Envy won't help, but you can use your anger to motivate yourself so that you can move up the organization and become a dallying boss too!

Think you are becoming adept at anger management? Then identify a second dirty dozen and apply what you know to clean them up.

VIOLENCE AT WORK

Shootings, stabbings, vandalism, threats, and aggressive behavior have become all-too-frequent occurrences at work. These violent acts are almost always initiated by mismanaged anger. To make matters worse, violence at work usually brings more violent acts, unless it is dealt with effectively.

What can be done? Here are my recommendations. First, it is imperative to recognize that the best intervention is to prevent the violence from occurring, rather than dealing with it after the fact.

Some recent studies show that violence at work can be deterred by increasing employee awareness about the subject. Thus, it is good policy to use awareness groups and printed material to educate employees about violence: what it is, how it differs from anger and conflict, why it happens, how to recognize potential acts and perpetrators of violence, and how to get individuals' input on how violence at work can best be handled. Make sure your information is accurate.

A second violence preventive is based on the fact that empirical research and models of violence indicate that learning to manage anger is perhaps the most crucial factor in preventing episodes of violence. Thus, training yourself and others in anger management skills seems to be essential and should be included in any training program designed to prevent and manage violence at work.

A third component of violence prevention is for organizations to institutionalize structures and systems that allow individuals to manage conflict. There is wide agreement that providing a forum for individuals to express their anger and work out conflicts with other individuals or with company policymakers is a deterrent to violence, probably because it validates the individuals' feelings and creates the perception that they have some control in the situation. A good start is to have an alternative dispute resolution

(ADR) procedure and to train all employees—not just managers—in conflict resolution skills, especially negotiation, mediation, and arbitration.

A fourth means of violence prevention is to examine your organization's culture. What attitude does your organization project to its employees? Does it foster positive affect, trust, and respect for the individual? Violence is often triggered by perceptions of injustice and feelings of depersonalization. Aim to have a culture that values fairness and support for all. Reward people who work within the system.

Fifth, organizations, especially human resource departments, need to recognize that recent changes in the world of work have set the stage for increased workplace aggression and violence by exposing millions of people to conditions that facilitate feelings of anger and aggressiveness. By increasing awareness of these factors, organizations can begin the process of managing the negative affect that accompanies these working-world realities. These factors, indentified by social psychologists, include downsizing and layoffs, work force diversity, affirmative action programs, and advances in technology.

The connection between downsizing and anger is an easy one to make. As for the others, work force diversity can be very positive, but only when diverse groups perceive some commonality among them. If diverse groups hold on to their rigid stereotyping of one another, and if the interaction among diverse groups tends to strengthen these stereotypes, anger and aggressive behaviors may intensify among them. Diversity may also pave the way for anger because ethnic or cultural differences often hinder interpersonal communication. For example, nonverbal cues such as eye contact and facial expressions are different across cultures, and members of these groups sometimes experience difficulty in interpreting one another's nonverbal cues. Interpersonal friction may be increased by the "noise" that diversity adds to the communication system.

Affirmative action programs offer plenty of positives, but the downside of such policies is resentment and anger on the part of those who feel that they have been passed over for promotion or other benefits they deserve in favor of a minority co-worker. These reactions are quite common, have been linked to reduced organizational commitment, and may very well increase aggressive behavior. It may also be that hardworking and talented members of minority groups sometimes resent affirmative action policies because they fear that their success will be falsely attributed to affirmative action pressures rather than to their own accomplishments. These fears are well grounded: Studies show that success on the part of women and minorities is often attributed to affirmative action policies in cases where they played no role. Thus, implementation of affirmative action policies may be a source of anger and frustration even for the persons who benefit from them.

Rapid technological advances also seem to intensify anger and aggression. These advances often greatly alter the nature of work processes or specific jobs, and many employees react to such change with negative emotions. This is the case with computer-based work monitoring. In such procedures, employees' performance is monitored continuously through the computers that they use in their work. Computer-based work monitoring, which is currently being used with more than ten million employees, has been found to induce strong feelings of anxiety and anger among employees, again increasing the likelihood of aggressive behavior.

Sixth, human resource and personnel departments can help by scrutinizing the mental health of their employees and organizations. Profiles of potentially violent employees can be established, and common denominators of situations that evoke violence can be determined. Sensing and assessing your organizational "mood" will help determine if you are in an environment where violence may be forthcoming. This information can be very helpful in designing appropriate training interventions. Additional human resource services that can be of help are crisis phone lines, strong EAP programs, and counseling services to family members of violent employees.

Despite your good intentions, violent acts still may occur. If a violent act occurs, it is imperative that you conduct "trauma group meetings" to help individuals process their feelings and concerns. These groups provide the crucial function of allowing individuals to verbalize how the violent incident has affected them and to listen to how others cope with similar feelings. Often, through group problem solving, individuals leave sessions with new insights and strategies for coping with violence on the job. At the very least, these groups communicate that the violence is recognized and that something is being done about it. There should also be follow-up group meetings, and, of course, individual counseling should be available.

A key factor for the effectiveness of trauma group meetings will be the training and clinical expertise of the individual leading the group. It would be a mistake to think that the skills for running a trauma group can be learned in a one-week course. If an organization does not have a qualified clinical psychologist, psychiatrist, or licensed counselor on board, the smart thing to do would be to bring in outside qualified individuals to do the job.

Violence at work is an issue that is now a frequent reality, so it is best to deal with it preventively. Now is the best time to do it.

Final Thoughts

Anger at Work **has brought together a wide body of knowledge for the** purpose of teaching you how to use anger productively on the job so that the quality of your work, work relationships, job enjoyment, and overall results improve. Many concepts and how-to examples have been presented, but beyond those specifics, I have a few conclusions I would like to leave with you.

There will always be anger because, like other feelings and emotions, it serves important roles in our lives and in the world. Anger is a cue that alerts us that something is wrong. It gives us information about people and situations. It brings to our attention injustices and abuse when they occur. These are valuable functions of anger that we cannot do without. Without anger, problems go unnoticed, situations become worse, injustice and abuse run rampant. In this sense, anger is intrinsically good. This is why people who wish a world without anger miss the point; what they really wish for is a world without injustice and abuse, two universal and timeless anger provokers. To be sure, without anger, there would be more abuse and injustice.

Anger that goes unrecognized is destined to be bad. It will disrupt our thoughts, cause us to act in inappropriate ways, and eventually become a poison in our system that makes it harder and harder to live productively. This is why self-awareness and awareness of others are so important—they prevent anger from going undetected as well as tuning us in to the moods of the moment.

When anger is detected and is still ignored, it becomes ugly as it seeks more and more extreme and usually violent ways to get attention. What else could you expect? If anger functions as a cue that something is wrong and that cue is ignored, then the anger is intensified so that it can be heard. If still disregarded, it becomes more intense until it can no longer be controlled.

This anger becomes deadly. For the individual, maybe a drinking or eating problem, or an on-the-job shooting. For the company, a strike. For the city, a riot. For the country, a revolution. For the world, a war. While it is true that much of this "ugly anger" changes the world for the better, it is hard to take the position that the end justifies the means. Surely, there are other options.

Finally, anger arouses us. On the micro level, it can potentiate a feeling of control. When a situation is getting out of hand, converting anger arousal into energy enables us to take charge and assert our will or interest. On a global level, it becomes the catalyst for change. Indeed, no one really needs examples of how the power of anger has changed the world.

Your final task is clear. It is to remember that anger has the capacity to be the good, the bad, and the ugly. It is up to each of us to maximize its good, minimize the bad, and eliminate the ugly.

References

Baron, R. *Workplace Violence and Aggression*. Forthcoming paper, Rensselaer Polytechnic Institute, Department of Managerial Policy & Organization.

Baron, R., and D. Byrne. *Social Psychology*. Boston: Allyn and Bacon, 1991.

Hadfield, E. *Emotional Contagion*. Unpublished paper, University of Hawaii, 1993.

McKay, M., M. Davis, and P. Fanning. *Thoughts and Feelings*. San Francisco: New Harbinger Publications, 1981. These authors developed the SOLVE acronym.

McKay, M., P. Rogers, and J. McKay. *When Anger Hurts*. San Francisco: New Harbinger Publications, 1989.

Madow, L. *Anger*. New York: Charles Scribner's Sons, 1972.

Sonkin, D., and M. Durphy. *Learning to Live Without Violence*. San Francisco: Volcano Press, 1982.

Weisinger, H. *The Critical Edge*. New York: HarperCollins Publishers, 1990.

Weisinger, H. *Dr. Weisinger's Anger Workout Book*. New York: William Morrow and Company, Inc., 1985.

Index

169

		DATE DUE		

JAMES PRENDERGAST
LIBRARY ASSOCIATION

JAMESTOWN, NEW YORK

Member Of

Chautauqua-Cattaraugus Library System